PASSIONATE RELATIONSHIP

ARVIND UPADHYAY

Copyright © Arvind Upadhyay
All Rights Reserved.

This book has been published with all efforts taken to make the material error-free after the consent of the author. However, the author and the publisher do not assume and hereby disclaim any liability to any party for any loss, damage, or disruption caused by errors or omissions, whether such errors or omissions result from negligence, accident, or any other cause.

While every effort has been made to avoid any mistake or omission, this publication is being sold on the condition and understanding that neither the author nor the publishers or printers would be liable in any manner to any person by reason of any mistake or omission in this publication or for any action taken or omitted to be taken or advice rendered or accepted on the basis of this work. For any defect in printing or binding the publishers will be liable only to replace the defective copy by another copy of this work then available.

we are going to explore, evaluate, and discover the secrets of bringing greater passion and fulfillment to your present relationship. And if you are not presently in a relationship, we will identify the skills and the qualities that will enable you to make a successful selection, avoid typical pitfalls, and develop the love of your life. We believe that nobody can enjoy a fulfilling relationship long-term without cultivating 7 Master Relationship Skills and observing the 10 Disciplines of Love and Passion. These are the essential skills and personal standards that will guide you to strengthen your relationship even during times of stress, uncertainty, and transition. The lessons you learn here and 7 Master Relationship Skills can be applied to any other relationships in your life as well. However, our core focus is really on the intimate relationship you have or want to create. This intimate relationship, as the emotional core of your life, will affect all of the other relationships in your life. Specifically, we will focus on three things: 1. How to create or rejuvenate an extraordinary, passionate relationship on all levels 2. How to deal with the inevitable challenges that show up 3. How to nurture and expand your relationship so you never stop growing and continue to experience greater joy, love, fulfillment, and passion You'll begin by listening to the 10-day audio program, which forms the backbone of this program. Days one and two will help you to understand your current personal relationships, define what kind of relationships you would like to enjoy in your life—whether or not you are with someone right now—and to summarize the foundational principles for making your relationship extraordinary. The remaining eight days are special on-the-spot interventions between Tony and individuals and couples at Tony's live seminars. Narrated by Cloé Madanes, each of these unique sessions focuses on cultivating one of the 7 essential relationship skills and the 10 core disciplines which create a compelling, heartfelt, loving, and passionate relationship. Relationship is complex and challenging, but we've designed this program with Tony and Sage to be nearly foolproof. If you develop these 7 Relationship Skills and practice the 10 Disciplines of Love and passion with a compatible partner, we believe your relationship must improve greatly! Thousands of individuals and couples have used this program to find the love of their lives. We invite you to try it, apply yourself, and create the relationship of your dreams!

how the 7 Relationship Skills and the 10 Disciplines are applied to your relationship to create results in real-life situations. We have found that when even one of these critical skills is lacking, it is the basis of upset, hurt, anger, frustration, and fear. When they are present, however, magic happens and an exemplary relationship is created and sustained. Many relationships have great foundations, but are brought lower because of a single "weak point"—a loss of passion, a point of chronic disagreement, or a problem trusting. The 7 Master Relationship Skills will help you to identify and address the weak points, bringing almost instantaneous improvement. Finally, while you will learn immensely from just listening to the audios and watching the films, it is crucial that you take action in your actual relationships. Follow Tony's assignment at the end of each audio, and use the pages that follow to answer lingering questions, brainstorm solutions, and discover life-altering distinctions. Each day's chapter begins with a scorecard of the 7 Relationship Skills, where you can sharpen your observations of that day's session. A second section will cover the main points to remember about that day's lesson and will give you helpful exercises to apply to your own life. Finally, each chapter concludes with assignment to you. Please make sure that, at the very least, you go to assignment at the end of each chapter—this is where your progress will be greatest. FOR SINGLES: This book is not only about improving present relationships—it is about finding a vision for your ideal relationship, strengthening yourself in communication, feeling, and awareness, avoiding the typical relationship obstacles, and taking essential steps towards fulfillment. The last thing you want is to repeat the mistakes of your past. Use the following exercises to understand your own past relationship patterns and to become the best person you can be, so that you can attract a partner of the same high quality.

Contents

1

DAY 1: LOVERS FOR LIFE: THE PATH OF LASTING PASSION

Relationships: There is perhaps no other word loaded in the English language with so many meanings, emotions, opinions, fears, heartbreak, or joy. Yet, there is nothing more important. We can have amazing kids, a great job, a fit body, financial abundance, emotional strength, and spiritual resolve and yet, without someone to share all of this with, it brings less meaning to our lives. If you've ever had the privilege of experiencing great love, you know firsthand the power it has to transform virtually every facet of your life. Extraordinary relationships are not the result of good luck, great chemistry, or convenience. Rather, there are laws of love—skills we need to hone, practice, and apply—which determine the amount of fulfillment we experience in our intimate lives. Specifically, the 7 Master Skills and the 10 Disciplines of Love and Passion are the backbone of this program, and create the base of any outstanding relationship. The ultimate key to creating and experiencing an extraordinary, fulfilling relationship, however, is to first work on you: to overcome your fears, to be more of who you really are at your core, and to master the skills and disciplines that will not only transform your relationships, but the quality of your entire life as well. When you raise your standard for what you expect from yourself in this area, you will naturally call out the best in your partner THE THREE LEVELS OF MASTERY To attain the level of mastery that will fulfill us at the deepest level, there are three levels we must achieve in any area of life:

LEVEL 1: Cognitive Understanding You understand it intellectually. LEVEL 2: Emotional Mastery You feel it emotionally. LEVEL 3: Physical Mastery You embody it and own it in your physiology. If you want to create substantial results in your life, mere knowledge is not enough. Anything you learn and want to apply to your life must go through several levels of mastery. Beginning with Cognitive Understanding, you have an insight about what works, what doesn't work, and what must be done to create the results you want. The next level is Emotional Mastery, when you feel emotionally the necessity of applying yourself to making this change real. However, the real results come with Physical Mastery, when you not only know and feel what must be done, but you repeatedly apply your knowledge to your life until it becomes a pattern in your body. For example, you may begin by understanding that a certain behavior of yours always creates friction and problems in relationships: let's say, a tendency to be controlling with your partner. You may even repeatedly feel that change is important enough to try a different direction in your relationship. However, it is not until you commit to, repeat, and condition a different approach in your life that you create a new relationship pattern that will bring permanent improvement. Passionate relationships are not for the lazy! When you encounter a relationship pattern in your life that needs to change, make sure that you take consistent massive action to create a new pattern in your relationship. For lasting change, take your understanding to the level of physical mastery. When you own something at Level 3, Physical Mastery becomes part of your identity. This is the only way for a transformation in any area of your life to last.

THE SIX POSITIONS OF RELATIONSHIPS Before you embark on any journey, it's a good idea to know where you're going. As we set off to create the ideal relationship, the first step is to understand where you are. In fact, everyone is in one of six positions in regards to relationship. Position One: A magnificent relationship with love and passion. This is what relationship is all about: all of the fun, spontaneity, intimacy, excitement, passion, closeness, and devotion. When you're in position one, you never want it to end. This is "the zone" for relationship! Position Two: A relationship with love, but little or no passion. You have a deep love with your partner, and your friends and family think you have a good, stable relationship. However, you no longer have the passion, juice, fun, and excitement you want. You feel more like family members than lovers. You may have had this passion in the past and grown comfortable, or you may not ever have had it in the first place. The good news is, it's possible to move from Position Two to Position One within minutes or seconds! This is an exciting place to be, as the rewards can be immediate. Position Three: A relationship with not much love, not much passion. You and your partner may live together, and you may be comfortable, but there is no deep emotional involvement. There may be friction between you, as neither of you feels very loved or wanted, or possibly you have each found ways to meet the majority of your needs outside of the relationship. If the great majority of your attention, focus, and interest is on work, hobbies, family (other than your partner), friends, etc., you are probably in Position Three. What's difficult about this position is that you may feel your partner is a good person—not good enough to get excited about, not bad enough to leave. However, this position shows a deterioration of the relationship and will only get worse as time goes by, unless you turn it around.

Position Four: You are planning your escape. You're with your partner, but you were in Position Three for so long that now you've got your finger on the button. You don't feel committed to making the relationship work, you're just waiting for the right conditions to leave. Maybe you're waiting for the kids to go to college, maybe you're waiting for finances to change. This position—where there is no love, friendship, or romance, and there is only procrastination and lying—can be extremely destructive for children to witness. You need to move up to Positions One and Two, or you need to make a move out of the relationship. The ULTIMATE RELATIONSHIP PROGRAM will support you with either decision—though you won't have your "final answer" until at least the tenth day. Either way, make a commitment and give yourself a deadline. The cost of staying in Position Four in the long term? A feeling that you never tasted what life is about, a lifetime of stress, fear, and rationalization. And a terrible example for your children of what life and relationship is about. Don't let your life slip away while you wait and delay. Position Five: You are out of a relationship, but want to be in one. You have either never been in a committed relationship, you've made your escape from a prior relationship, or your partner has left you. You may have been in this position for some time, concerned about repeating the experiences of your prior relationship. While this position holds much pain for most people, it is also a place of opportunity. The ULTIMATE RELATIONSHIP PROGRAM will help you to clarify the kind of relationship you want and the kind of shifts and actions that will get you there. If you are getting over the loss of a previous relationship, be careful that you don't start to take on beliefs that will be destructive to future possible relationships. It's tempting to make generalizations about the opposite sex, or the type of person or relationship you were with before. Instead, develop a checklist for what you did and didn't do in that previous relationship. If you work on yourself, clarify your priorities, and take the proven steps in this program, you will be headed towards Position One very soon!

Position Six: You are out of a relationship, and don't want to be in one. While this position may be comfortable, private, and consistent, you are missing out on one of the greatest emotional experiences of life! Ask yourself: do you really want to live and die alone? Do you never want to be loved and worshiped by a lover whom you love and worship? We believe that love is the prime motivation and the prime area of spiritual growth for human beings. It is tempting to rationalize and say that you don't need relationship—but that is usually just fear. If you're in Position Six, you need to see some new examples of how relationship can be. Watch the films and see the turnarounds. If you really think you never want a relationship again, at least complete the entire ten day program before making that decision. Give yourself ten days to witness what can be possible in relationship, then make up your mind.

Notes

DO IT NOW: DAY 1 ASSIGNMENT Be Honest . . . 1. What is your ultimate vision for your intimate relationship? What do you want to create, give, have, share and become in this area of your life? What is your compelling vision for love, intimacy, passion, connection, and fun? Describe the relationship, not the partner.

"Love is a condition in which the happiness of another person is essential to your own." —Robert Heinlein

2. Which of the six relationship positions are you really in?

3. If you're in a relationship, which position is your partner in? Why do you think so? What have you felt or observed?

4. What has been preventing you from taking your relationship to the next level? What beliefs, behavior patterns, or emotions have held you back from taking the next step?

5. What would it take to change it all? What fears, beliefs, or past memories can you transform to go to the next level? What do you need to do now to create the relationship you desire and deserve?

Notes

2

DAY 2: THE SECRETS TO OUTSTANDING RELATIONSHIPS: THE 7 MASTER SKILLS & THE 10 DISCIPLINES OF LOVE

What makes a relationship extraordinary? The truth is there are many factors that play into the textures, dance, and quality of human relations. A truly magnificent love affair is the result of the commitment to a daily practice: the ongoing mastery of the fundamental skills necessary for an extraordinary relationship and the disciplines to hold yourself, your thoughts, and your actions to the standards that bring out the best in you and your partner. "The day will come when, after harnessing the winds, the tides and gravitation, we shall harness for God the energies of love. And on that day, for the second time in the history of the world, man will have discovered fire." —Teilhard de Chardin 7 SKILLS AND 10 DISCIPLINES The 7 Master Relationship Skills and the 10 Disciplines of Love are the laws of love: the rules for creating a legendary relationship. The universe operates according to certain laws. If we don't pay heed to these laws, we get the same consequence every time. If we ignore the law of gravity, we will fall. We believe the 7 Relationship Skills and the 10 Disciplines are the natural laws of intimate relationships. If you choose to ignore these skills and disciplines, it's like ignoring the law of gravity, and there's a price to be paid for that. Every relationship requires these 7 Relationship Skills, whether it's a friendship, a family relationship, or an intimate relationship. However, sometimes skills are not enough. In order to enjoy and magnify any relationship to the fullest, you also need high standards: a set of daily disciplines for how you will show up in that relationship no matter what. If you consistently apply the Master Relationship Skills and live the Disciplines of Love, you will create a legendary relationship filled with joy, passion, fun, ecstasy, and love.

Heartfelt Understanding When anything is perceived to be more important than your partner, the relationship is not going to go to the ultimate depth of love. Understand and empathize with your partner's emotional patterns and commit to being there for them. Give Your Partner What They Really Need As long as you're focusing on what you're not getting, you're never going to be in a place of being a giver, which is what makes a relationship grow. The only love that you get to feel is the love that you give. And the love that you hold back, that's the love that you'll never have in your life. What would you give to someone you love? The answer is everything. Create and Build Trust and Respect Trust begins with commitment to your partner's needs. Can your partner depend on you to be emotionally available no matter what, even in times of stress and uncertainty? You can't separate these two, because trust is based on commitment. Reclaim Playfulness, Presence, and Passion Polarity doesn't age. You can spark passion in your lover that has been dormant for years. It can take minutes. What does your partner need? Who are you at your core? How can you express your deepest gift to your partner? Harness Courage and Embrace Honesty We are all rewarded and discouraged for certain behaviors in our relationships. We all have needs and fears which constrain us from doing and saying everything that we feel. When we don't express ourselves in the moment, we start to hold back, which leads to less passion. Have the courage to break through constricting beliefs and fears and express yourself with passion. Uncover and Create Alignment The worst thing on earth is to be in a relationship where you have completely different needs and goals. Your beliefs don't have to be identical, but they have to lead you in the same direction. Live Consciously: Be an Example Don't be your history; don't just imitate your parent's examples. Create your own example. The best way to transform your family group is to transform yourself—the change will spread through generations. Do it for yourself and for the others who will learn from you!

THE 10 DISCIPLINES OF LOVE The Discipline of Putting Your Lover First: It's Not About You! Put your lover's feelings and needs first. When you are feeling pain you are focused on yourself. The Discipline of Loving No Matter What: The Power of Love, Adoration, & Praise Withholding your gift is the only source of pain. With real love, you love through pain, joy, fear. Love penetrates all. The Discipline of Being Yourself: Emanate & Express Your Natural Essence & True Core You can't align with someone if you're not being yourself or if you're trying to be what you think they want. You have to tell the truth! Playing small never serves. The Discipline of Positive Intent: Eliminate Threats & Judgment & Remember The Power of Language Never make your partner wrong. Know their soul. The Discipline of Freedom: The Power of Forgiving, Forgetting, & Flooding Pain can only be found in yesterday's sorrows or tomorrow's concerns. Flood yourself now with the beauty and magic of your life! The Discipline of Daily Intimacy: Full Engagement— Open Your Heart & Hold Nothing Back Play wildly, courageously, tenderly, and intensely. Fear and hurt imprison the heart. Do the opposite of what they tell you and passion will re-ignite. The Discipline of Polarity: The Power of Dancing Energies Feel, understand, and appreciate what your partner needs and serve them now. Be her mountain. Presence is a state where nothing shakes you. Be his joy. Playfulness is the gift of life. Give your gift. The Discipline of Loving Truth: The Power of Vulnerability Give the gift of heartfelt honesty and commit to expressing it openly in this moment. The Discipline of Utilization: The Power of Higher Meaning & Constant Growth Find the good and beauty in everything and use it to expand your love. The Discipline of Gratitude & Giving: Appreciation is the Power Experience life's greatest blessings now.

SKILL 1: HEARTFELT UNDERSTANDING This is not just intellectual understanding, not being condescending or judging your partner's needs and behaviors. Heartfelt Understanding is about connecting to your partner's emotional world and putting yourself in his or her shoes. If someone doesn't feel understood at the heart level by his or her partner, the relationship can hardly make progress from there. On the other hand, you'd be amazed at how much a relationship can change when one of the partners decides to give complete heartfelt understanding without judgment. Does heartfelt understanding mean that you have to agree with your partner on everything? No, of course not—but it shows them that you are on their side. How do you know whether you have heartfelt understanding for your partner? We don't want these skills to be intellectual concepts, we want to apply them and create real results in our lives. In order to develop the first skill of Heartfelt Understanding to the utmost, you must make it a daily discipline . . . "It is well to give when asked but it is better to give unasked, through understanding." —Kahlil Gibran DISCIPLINE 1: PUTTING YOUR LOVER FIRST: IT'S NOT ABOUT YOU! When you develop the skill of heartfelt understanding fully, you become fully conscious of your partner's inner life. Rather than being your partner's observer and critic, you find that "inner heart connection": you feel what they feel. Practice being selfless—schedule periods of time where you will attend to your partner's needs, putting your needs second or third. Tune in to your partner's responses. What do they like? What doesn't score points? Refine your approach. What gifts, gestures, touch or words strike a chord in your partner? How can you become even more proficient in loving and pleasing him or her? It is by putting your lover first that you will discover the deepest pleasure in your relationship—sexual and other.

SKILL 2: GIVE YOUR PARTNER WHAT THEY REALLY NEED In any relationship, you have to be aware of the other person's needs in order to know what's going on. Not knowing your partner's needs inevitably leads to frustration and disappointment, where you are giving your partner everything except what they really need. The challenge with people is that their deepest needs are often incredibly specific and can be tricky to discern—it's like a "secret button". If you never find your partner's "secret button," the relationship will feel impossible. The good news is that if you can find the secret button and figure out how to give your partner what they need at the deepest level, you can generate levels of trust, happiness, love, and passion more profoundly than anything either of you has ever experienced. The fact is that everybody has the same 6 Human Needs (which will be discussed at length in day 3). You discover how that person meets their needs, you'll know how to satisfy them. To make it a consistent practice, however, you must apply Discipline 2 . . . DISCIPLINE 2: LOVING NO MATTER WHAT: THE POWER OF LOVE, ADORATION, & PRAISE One of the biggest threats to any relationship is when one or both partners withdraw from each other. Loving No Matter What is a commitment to hold yourself open and present for your lover, even during the most painful of situations. Anytime that you withdraw emotionally, even in a subtle way, from your partner, the relationship deteriorates. Any time that you lose trust, interest, and commitment, even for a moment, you drift closer to behaviors of criticism and rejection. The good news is that if you commit to maintaining your emotional connection, no matter what, there will never be any room for alienation, judgment, and rejection. Stay connected! Cultivate your connection and your commitment the way you would cultivate a precious flower! If you commit to love your partner no matter what and hold to this crucial discipline, your relationship will flourish no matter what your life circumstances may be.

DISCIPLINE 3: BEING YOURSELF: EMANATE & EXPRESS YOUR NATURAL ESSENCE & TRUE CORE If the basis of trust is confidence in your partner, then trust must begin with having confidence in yourself. If you cannot trust who you yourself are at your deepest level, you cannot induce lasting trust in others. Having confidence means having confidence in your own highest intentions and commitment—trusting yourself to do the right thing. When you have the self-trust of being yourself, emanating your natural essence, others will perceive that and build trust in you. Being yourself also means that you recognize the masculine and feminine energies that form you. You may have an intense masculine energy that you've always been discouraged from expressing. In a relationship of heartfelt understanding, giving, and trust, you can learn how to reclaim those parts of you that you may have suppressed. If you have ever felt feminine energies that have been seen as inefficient or misdirected, you can learn to embrace and appreciate them. Energies of gender and sexuality are intense topics in our culture, and we have been taught that many of these energies are wrong—as a result, we get to experience less in life. Allow these energies to enhance you in your intimacy and your life's purpose, and recognize and appreciate these energies in your partner. Finally, being yourself also means trusting your own intent. If you have decided to put your lover first, trust that commitment—if your partner challenges or tests you (as will happen, anytime you make a change to the status quo in your relationship) hold true to the generosity of your own intentions.

SKILL 3: CREATE AND BUILD TRUST AND RESPECT Trust is the essential building block of every productive relationship in your life. Where there is no trust, people do not share, and where they do not share, there is no interaction, progress, or common growth. Trust comes from the feeling that you have common interests—namely, that you are committed to meeting each others' needs. Trust is not built during the easy times, but during times of uncertainty and stress, when your commitment to your partner comes under question. When your commitment withstands these tests, your trust will expand and grow to new levels, giving you new levels of freedom, comfort, and love. When you fail to grow trust, you can only lose it. There's no middle ground. In fact, there are 3 Disciplines to master in order to foster ongoing trust and respect . . .

DISCIPLINE 4: POSITIVE INTENT: ELIMINATE THREATS & JUDGMENT & REMEMBER THE POWER OF LANGUAGE The basis of trust is the feeling that both of you have positive intent towards each other. Anytime you use threats, judgment, or humor as a weapon, you are undermining that feeling—and you are undermining the relationship itself. When you judge, threaten, or blame, you are presupposing that your partner's problem behavior is intentional and malicious. That puts them in an uncomfortably defensive position that can kill intimacy. At the same time, by judging, threatening, and blaming, you are demonstrating your own lack of faith in the relationship. Eliminating threats and judgments is one way of following through on your commitment to your partner. On the other hand, if your partner is upset, it is important to remember that behind your partner's upset feelings, there are needs that are not being met. If you can understand your partner's upsets with heartfelt compassion and empathy, you will preserve your connection and your trust. Awaken to the power of language, praise, and verbal affection. So many relationships wither and die simply because the partners never learned how to communicate their true feelings to each other! Discover the words and language that stimulate and please your partner! Don't be afraid to repeat yourself! This is a daily discipline that needs to be reinforced several times every day.

DISCIPLINE 5: FREEDOM: THE POWER OF FORGIVING, FORGETTING, & FLOODING Every relationship undergoes times of hardship and stress, and people often make mistakes. Knowing that, why drag along the baggage of past sufferings and mistakes? Whenever we have painful experiences or memories, we have a choice: to either learn from them, or use them to punish ourselves or others. So often people imprison their partners with guilt and blame for their past misdeeds. That never creates intimacy. If you want passion, set your partner free of guilt and blame. Make your choice—if you are putting your partner first, then truly forgive them. See their mistake from their perspective. Now, some things are not easy to forget—sometimes we get locked into old memories and linger there, experiencing resentment and anxiety. In this case, use the strategy of "flooding," which is a way of working with your own mind and nervous system to replace bad experiences with good. This doesn't mean senselessly forgetting important lessons and warnings from the past—it's a way of consciously harnessing the good in life and bringing it into yourself for greater pleasure and intimacy. Flooding means consciously reliving the good in your life, bringing up memories and feelings of love, gratitude, and appreciation. If you strengthen these emotions purposefully—and it may feel at first that you are "faking" these new emotional patterns—they will take root in your body and nervous system, and soon you will begin to experience these emotions spontaneously. You'll see that most of the interventions in this program reach a point where the couple must undergo forgiving, forgetting, and flooding in order to reach a solution.

SKILL 4: RECLAIM PLAYFULNESS, PRESENCE, AND PASSION Many couples achieve—or rebuild—a basis of heartfelt understanding, giving, and trust, but aren't able to make the leap to passion and excitement. In Skill 4, we reclaim the playfulness, presence, and passion that is in every human being's soul—and which can awaken your relationship to the level of passion you may not have experienced for years. In a relationship where there is heartfelt understanding, giving, and trust, the partners need to take the next step, where they play with their partner. If you are masculine, this would mean showing your passion, pursuing, and initiating lovemaking with your partner. If you are feminine, this would mean playfully provoking and enticing your partner to come after you. Playfully exaggerate your gender differences—that will certainly stimulate the polarity between you. In sexual intimacy, open up the spectrum of experiences to embrace not only the light emotions (loyalty, contribution, devotion) but also the dark emotions (naughtiness, possessiveness, lust). If you have heartfelt understanding, selflessness, and trust in your relationship, why not enjoy the fruits of it? Open up, experiment, take a risk, and enjoy! Follow the disciplines of intimacy and polarity to make playfulness, presence, and passion part of your daily experience . . . DISCIPLINE 6: THE DISCIPLINE OF DAILY INTIMACY : FULL ENGAGEMENT—OPEN YOUR HEART AND HOLD NOTHING BACK Once you seek out, discover, and appreciate your natural polarity with your partner, let that passion and excitement infiltrate the other parts of your life. Open your heart to your partner, and let your presence, playfulness, and passion bring spice to your times together. Don't hold back. Be present with your partner. If there were times that you used to shut down or look the other way, engage your partner in those times and communicate. Relationships must be fed with honesty and attention. When you open your heart and create this level of connection and enjoyment, your relationship will have a solid base that can weather any storm.

DISCIPLINE 7: THE DISCIPLINE OF POLARITY : THE POWER OF DANCING ENERGIES Opposites attract. We all know it, but we don't always know why. In science, the attraction of opposites is called polarity, which can be found in electricity, magnetism, and other physical phenomena. In human relationship, many types of polarity can be observed—we are naturally attracted to those things and people which are different from us and which stimulate us in ways we cannot stimulate ourselves. You may have a friend who is funnier than you and is attractive in that way, for instance. That creates spontaneous attraction and respect. In romantic intimacy, polarity refers to the play between opposite energies—the masculine and the feminine. Those are the energies behind sex and gender, and they are responsible for sexual attraction and passion as well. The good news is that it is not our external looks, age, or social position that creates passion! Passion is not a naturally fading phenomenon. Sexual polarity is an eternal energy, and is responsible for great sex and lasting passion. If you can find your natural polarity with your partner—the play of differences between you—you can sustain a magnetic attraction or rediscover the passion that you may have experienced long ago. One way to increase polarity is to take on the strengths of your gender—if you are masculine, the strengths of purpose, protection, and commitment. If you are feminine, the strengths of vulnerability, the flow of feeling, spontaneity, and provocative play. Play on your respective strengths, even exaggerate your differences, until the polarity sparks. It's okay to feel an aspect of pretend and experimentation. The place where polarity is strongest, however, is in the difficult times of stress and upset. In those times, utilize the strengths of your sexual essence to help your partner! If you are masculine, stand strong, give your partner your devotion and commitment, no matter what they say or do. If you are feminine, heal your partner with your love, attention, and provoke them with your playfulness. Polarity is one of those things that strengthens relationships, no matter what they are going through—as you'll see in the films and audio sessions. Find your polarity, and you'll have not only love and trust, but passion as well.

SKILL 5: HARNESS COURAGE AND EMBRACE HONESTY Once you have passion and polarity, you will have intense enjoyment, and you will also have moments of surprise, hurt, and disappointment. It comes with every human relationship, and an exceptional romance is no exception. In these times, what will feed and maintain your heartfelt understanding, giving, trust, and passion is the truth. When things are going well and something upsets you, it's tempting to suppress it, not wanting to disturb the peace. But these upsets need to be dealt with in the moment, or else they build up and become unmanageable. In these moments, you need to harness your courage and embrace honesty, you need to share your experience with your partner. To do this, you must live the discipline of loving truth ...

SKILL 6: UNCOVER AND CREATE ALIGNMENT Are you truly compatible with your partner, or do you belong somewhere else? Will you ever be able to experience your authentic selves together with passion, or are your interests just too different? It's true that selection is a crucial part of relationship. Every relationship undergoes a time of investigation, checking, and re-evaluation. On day 10, you'll learn the key questions that define your compatibility with your partner, but you'll also learn an even greater skill. Once you understand the differences between you and your partner, you have a choice to make: whether to commit to your partner for the long term, or end the relationship and reselect another partner. If you choose to commit, the skill of alignment is about recognizing and appreciating your differences so that they enrich your lives rather than creating friction. Finding alignment with real situations—with all of their quirks and surprises—is one of the keys to fulfillment in life. Uncovering and creating alignment with a partner you love and desire, with all their challenges and needs, is the path of greatest growth in relationship.

DISCIPLINE 8: THE DISCIPLINE OF LOVING TRUTH: THE POWER OF VULNERABILITY This is not only a discipline, but an art—of expressing mild upset without creating even bigger upset. When something bothers you and you explain this, your partner will have a tendency to feel blamed. However, the fact is that when something goes wrong, you must express yourself spontaneously, in the moment, and from the heart. In order to do this successfully, it is crucial that you set the context carefully for anything you are about to share. When approaching your partner with this type of feedback, remember to use the phrases which avoid blame and save face. You will learn these in the chapter for days 3 and 9

DISCIPLINE 9: THE DISCIPLINE OF UTILIZATION: THE POWER OF HIGHER MEANING & CONSTANT GROWTH You have two choices of what to do with anything life (or your partner) gives you. You can either punish yourself or your partner with it, suffer, and feel pain, or you can decide to learn from it and apply it to your future. Choose the second option—learning, adapting, and enjoying is what we are designed for! When you have conflicts or misunderstandings with your partner, choose to learn, appreciate, embrace differences, and change your approach. This is the path of ultimate growth!

DISCIPLINE 10: THE DISCIPLINE OF GRATITUDE & GIVING: APPRECIATION IS POWER If the 7 Master Relationship Skills begin with committing to your partner and making them feel safe, the skills end with the ability to enjoy and appreciate your differences as well. So often our relationships are dampened by a false sense of familiarity and habit, making us forget what's most important—that your lover is the unique person in the world who is closest to you, that you are the bearer of special knowledge of your lovers' innermost secrets, desires, and individuality. Appreciate that! Get some perspective! Loving and appreciating your life partner is a great way to love and appreciate your life.

SKILL 7: LIVE CONSCIOUSLY: BE AN EXAMPLE If we were to examine our beliefs and behavior patterns under a microscope, we would find that a great deal of what we do and believe was not chosen consciously. Many of our appetites, desires, opinions, and behavior patterns were absorbed unconsciously at an early age from the people around us—our parents, family, and siblings. So many of us wake up one day to find that we have the habits or the relationship or the lifestyle of our father or mother, even if we never chose that. Default versions of how to live and how to love are the way many of us live our lives, and when we try to make a shift, we often meet resistance from others. The Skill of Living Consciously is the skill of applying yourself to all the relationship skills and disciplines— to have the courage to create a new example in your life of what is possible. Breaking out of age-old patterns takes discipline, focus, and consistency—as well as playfulness, passion, and the ability to handle surprise!

DO IT NOW: DAY 2 ASSIGNMENT Score yourself and explain why you gave yourself this score. How have you created these 7 Relationship Skills in your life? What would your relationship be like if you were observing these disciplines in your life? If you are not presently in a couple, how did you create these in a former relationship or with someone close to you? 1. SKILL: HEARTFELT UNDERSTANDING · Generate loving insight into your partner's needs, desires, and fears. Understand and empathize with your partner's emotional patterns and commit to being there for them. Score yourself (out of 10):

Do you follow The First Discipline of Putting Your Lover First?

2. SKILL: GIVE YOUR PARTNER WHAT THEY REALLY NEED Score yourself (out of 10)

3. SKILL: CREATE AND BUILD TRUST AND RESPECT Score yourself (out of 10):

Do you follow the second Discipline of Loving No Matter What: The Power of Love, Adoration, and Praise?

Do you follow the third Discipline of Being Yourself: Emanate and Express Your Natural Essence and True Core?

Do you follow the fourth Discipline of Positive Intent: Eliminate Threats and Judgment and Remember the Power of Language?

Do you follow the fifth Discipline of Freedom: The Power of Forgiving, Forgetting, and Flooding?

4. SKILL: RECLAIM PLAYFULNESS, PRESENCE, AND PASSION Score yourself (out of 10)

Do you follow the sixth Discipline of Daily Intimacy: Full Engagement—Open Your Heart and Hold Nothing Back?

Do you follow the seventh Discipline of Polarity: The Power of Dancing Energies?

SKILL: HARNESS COURAGE AND EMBRACE HONESTY Score yourself (out of 10):

6. SKILL: UNCOVER AND CREATE ALIGNMENT Score yourself (out of 10):

Do you follow the eighth Discipline of Loving Truth: The Power of Vulnerability?

Do you follow the tenth Discipline of Gratitude and Giving: Appreciation is the Power?

7. SKILL: LIVE CONSCIOUSLY: BE AN EXAMPLE Score yourself (out of 10)

Out of the Mouths of Babes When is it okay to kiss someone? "The rule goes like this: if you kiss someone, then you should marry them and have kids with them. It's the right thing to do."

Back From the Edge: Creating Everlasting Love

Do you follow the ninth Discipline of Utilization: The Power of Higher Meaning and Constant Growth?

3

DAY 3: BACK FROM THE EDGE: CREATING EVERLASTING LOVE

Today's message is an example of the transformation that occurs when two partners in a couple learn how to meet each others needs. Paul and Jenn were both good people and loved each other, but they were miserable. By renewing their commitment to each other and understanding the power of the 6 Human Needs, they were able to turn their relationship around in one day. Today we will explore the power of the 6 Human Needs—how to identify your most valued needs, as well as your partner's most valued needs and how to fulfill them. When you know how to meet your needs and your partner's needs, the keys of the relationship kingdom are yours. SCORE PAUL AND JENN ON THE 7 MASTER RELATIONSHIP SKILLS If you've seen or listened to Tony's conversation with Paul and Jenn, you'll remember some of the strengths and weaknesses of that relationship. In order to practice your skills of observation and strengthen your understanding of the 7 Master Relationship Skills, take a moment to score Paul and Jenn on their mastery of the 7 Skills. How did they start off the conversation? What did they learn? And how did they use what they learned that day to create the relationship they enjoy today? What did you learn about your own life?

SKILL 1: HEARTFELT UNDERSTANDING Paul's Score:_____ What did Paul understand about Jenn?

What did Paul not understand in a heartfelt way?

Paul's Score: How did Paul learn to understand Jenn better? How will that lead to action?

Jenn's Score: What kind of understanding did Jenn have of Paul? Did Paul feel understood by Jenn?

Why? How did that change?

How did Paul learn to meet Jenn's needs?

Jenn's Score:Which needs was Jenn meeting for Paul? Which was she not meeting?

How did Jenn learn to meet Paul's needs?

SKILL 3: CREATE AND BUILD TRUST AND RESPECT Paul's Score:_____ What could Jenn trust in Paul? What could she not trust?

What did Paul do to decrease trust? At the end of the day, what did he do to increase trust?

Jenn's Score: What could Paul trust about Jenn?

Did Paul feel trusted by Jenn?

What did Paul learn?

Jenn's Score: How playful was Jenn? Was she being playful in a way that inspired passion? Why or why not?

How did she learn to create more passion and playfulness with Paul?

SKILL 4: RECLAIM PLAYFULNESS, PRESENCE, AND PASSION Paul's Score:_____ Was Paul giving Jenn his full presence? Was he creating an emotional basis for Jenn to feel passion? What challenges did he have?

SKILL 5: HARNESS COURAGE AND EMBRACE HONESTY Paul's Score:_____ Where did Paul demonstrate courage and honesty? If he had not been courageous and honest enough to stand up and tell the truth, where would he be now?

What kinds of courage and honesty did Paul need to learn?

Every couple has differences. How did Paul create alignment despite these differences?

Jenn's Score: How were Jenn's relationships and loyalties strengthening or weakening her alignment with Paul?

What did she do to create greater alignment?

SKILL 7: LIVE CONSCIOUSLY: BE AN EXAMPLE Paul's Score: What kind of example had Paul been living for his family and children?

What had to change within Paul for him to live consciously as an example to others?

Jenn's Score: What positive or negative examples of relationship was Jenn using as an example for her own relationship?

What did Jenn have to do to create a new example of love in her life?

Do you know any couples or individuals like Paul and Jenn? What did you learn from Paul and Jenn's example?

1. CERTAINTY Certainty that we can be comfortable—to have pleasure and to avoid pain. 2. UNCERTAINTY/VARIETY Variety and challenges which will exercise our emotional and physical range. 3. SIGNIFICANCE Every person needs to feel special, important, needed, wanted.

4. LOVE/CONNECTION Everyone needs connection with other human beings and everyone strives for and hopes for love. 5. GROWTH When we stop growing, we die. We need to constantly develop emotionally, intellectually, and spiritually. 6. CONTRIBUTION To go beyond your own needs and give to others. Everything in the universe contributes beyond itself or it is eliminated.

We need to meet them every day, in one way or another. The good news is that there are only six of them. There are many ways of meeting them, and they don't cost money.

DO IT NOW: DAY 3 ASSIGNMENT The 6 Human Needs are the most effective way to track the level of happiness and fulfillment in any human relationship. Take a moment to score the way needs are met in your relationship. FOR SINGLES: Instead of focusing on a present relationship, take a moment to understand a past relationship or another important relationship in your life. By understanding and appreciating the past, you will build your future. Complete exercises 1 and 2, then skip to the SINGLES ONLY questions at the bottom. 1. Score yourself—from your partner's perspective—on how you have been meeting your partner's needs. Certainty/Comfort Your Score:

Why?

Name three ways you could meet this need for your partner

Uncertainty/Variety Your Score:_____ Why?

Name three ways you could meet this need for your partner.

Significance Your Score: Why?

Name three ways you could meet this need for your partner

Connection/Love Your Score: Why?

Name three ways you could meet this need for your partner.

Growth Your Score: Why?

Name three ways you could meet this need for your partner.

Contribution Your Partner's Score:_____ Why?

Name three ways you could meet this need for your partner.

Rank your partner's 6 Needs in order of importance to him or her, number one being most important (again, the needs are Certainty/Comfort, Uncertainty/Variety, Significance, Connection/ Love, Growth, and Contribution). 1.

2.

3.

4.

5.

6.

Certainty/Comfort Your Partner's Score:_____ Why?

Name three ways your partner could meet this need for you.

Uncertainty/Variety Your Partner's Score: Why?

Name three ways your partner could meet this need for you

Significance Your Partner's Score:_____ Why?

Name three ways your partner could meet this need for you.

Connection/Love Your Partner's Score:_____ Why?

Name three ways your partner could meet this need for you.

Growth Your Partner's Score:_____ Why?

Name three ways your partner could meet this need for you.

Contribution Your Partner's Score:_____ Why?

Name three ways your partner could meet this need for you.

Rank your 6 Human Needs in order of importance to you (number one being most important). 1.

2.

3.

_______________________________________ 4.

_______________________________________ 5.

____

_______________________________________ 6.

"You got to find somebody who likes the same stuff. Like, if you like sports, she should like it that you like sports, and she should keep the chips and dip coming."

3. Ask your partner how he or she would like to have their needs met. Discover your partner's preferences. What has to happen for him or her to experience that those top three needs are being met? What are the rules that govern their experience? For example, in order to feel loved, does your partner need a hug each day, or several hugs? Some time with you alone together? A phone call to express caring? Get specific. The more specific you get the easier it will be to discover the triggers that lead to satisfying your

partner's needs thereby deepening love, attraction and understanding.

Be aware that your partner may be modest and say that everything is fine. Human needs are among the most sensitive and intimate topics of conversation. Make it clear to your partner that they cannot hurt your feelings on this—you really want to know what you can do for them! Make your partner feel safe. Share your ideas of ways to meet their needs. Observe their responses.

4. Share what you would appreciate from your partner. Be aware that your partner may interpret this as a trade-off: "Since I gave you yours, now you owe me mine." If this is a concern, wait until another day or occasion to bring this up with your partner. Make sure to phrase your needs with humility, love, and respect. Share your list with your partner, and brain storm ways of meeting your needs.

SINGLES ONLY: What did you learn about the way you had met your partner's needs in the past? About the way your needs were or were not met? What is your new standard for meeting needs in relationship? How would you communicate your needs to your partner? How would you inquire into your partner's deepest needs?

4

DAY 4: BREAKING THROUGH: CREATING THE LIFE THAT YOU DESERVE

"Deep within man dwell those slumbering powers; powers that would astonish him, that he never dreamed of possessing; forces that would revolutionize his life if aroused and put into action." —Orison Swett Marden

So often our partners' emotional patterns are a mystery to us. One day they are happy and passionate, the next day—they are grumpy and shut down. Here you will learn the fundamental principles Tony uses in understanding the beliefs, behaviors, and challenges of anyone he meets. If you've seen or heard Tony's conversation with Tahnee, you've understood how Tahnee's moods—and even her problems—served to meet her 6 Human Needs in destructive ways. Among other things, here you'll find answers here to questions about depression, anger, mood swings, what holds us back from intimacy, and what keeps us from making the strong decisions we need in life. Today's Master Relationship Skill is Heartfelt Understanding. Every relationship begins with the partners' ability to empathize and understand each others needs, emotions, and situation. Today's Discipline of Love is the Discipline of Putting Your Lover first: It's Not About You! We'll see how Tahnee's focus on her own needs was actually the barrier to finding fulfillment with her boyfriend. Once she got out of her own way and made the leap of faith, she gained the life of her dreams.

1. Heartfelt Understanding 2. Give Your Partner What They Really Need 3. Create and Build Trust and Respect 4. Reclaim Playfulness, Presence, and Passion 5. Harness Courage and Embrace Honesty 6. Uncover and Create Alignment 7. Live Consciously: Be An Example (Skill 7 applies to all 10 Disciplines of Love) The 7 Master Skills The 10 Disciplines of Love 1. The Discipline of Putting Your Lover First: It's Not About You! 2. The Discipline of Loving No Matter What: The Power of Love, Adoration & Praise 3. The Discipline of Being Yourself: Emanate & Express Your Natural Essence & True Core 4. Discipline of Positive Intent: Eliminate Threats & Judgment & Remember The Power of Language 5. The Discipline of Freedom: The Power of Forgiving, Forgetting & Flooding 6. The Discipline of Daily Intimacy: Full Engagement—Open Your Heart & Hold Nothing Back 7. The Discipline of Polarity: The Power of Dancing Energies 8. The Discipline of Loving Truth: The Power of Vulnerability 9. The Discipline of Utilization: The Power of Higher Meaning & Constant Growth 10. The Discipline of Gratitude & Giving: Appreciation is the Power

SCORE TAHNEE ON THE 7 MASTER RELATIONSHIP SKILLS We did not meet Tahnee's boyfriend, did we? But let's challenge ourselves and try to understand how Tahnee would have scored in the 7 Master Relationship Skills. SKILL 1: HEARTFELT UNDERSTANDING Tahnee's Score:_____ Did Tahnee understand herself? Did she show any understanding of her boyfriend's needs?

What did she learn?

SKILL 2: GIVE YOUR PARTNER WHAT THEY REALLY NEED Tahnee's Score:_____ What did Tahnee talk about giving to her boyfriend? What was her focus?

Where do you think she ran into problems?

What did she learn?

SKILL 3: CREATE AND BUILD TRUST AND RESPECT Tahnee's Score:_____ How much trust did she have in her relationship? What kinds of challenges would you expect to see in a relationship that had that level of trust?

What did she learn?

What did she learn?

SKILL 4: RECLAIM PLAYFULNESS, PRESENCE, AND PASSION Tahnee's Score:_____ Did she experience a change in terms of her playfulness? How did that relate to the amount of passion that she was capable of experiencing?

What did she learn?

SKILL 5: HARNESS COURAGE AND EMBRACE HONESTY Tahnee's Score:_____ How honest was she being with herself about what her real challenges were? Was she working on a quality problem in her life, or was she struggling with a self-imposed problem? What needs was she meeting?

What did she learn?

SKILL 6: UNCOVER AND CREATE ALIGNMENT Tahnee's Score:_____ What kind of alignment would you expect her to have with her boyfriend? What kind of alignment did she experience once she created more trust, giving, courage, and made new life decisions?

What did she learn?

SKILL 7: LIVE CONSCIOUSLY: BE AN EXAMPLE Tahnee's Score:_____ Was she consciously creating a new example for those around her, or was she living in reaction to the examples of others?

When she made life changes after the conversation, what kind of example did she live?

"No age is good to get married at. You got to be a fool to get married." —Freddie, age 6

WHAT DID YOU LEARN? MAIN POINTS TO REMEMBER: EMOTION: THE FUEL OF CHOICE Emotions do not just happen to us. We "do" emotions. Emotions are formed by a triad: · Physiology—your posture, breathing, level of energy and/or tension · Focus—what are you choosing to focus on? · Language—what do you say to yourself on a regular basis? Alter any one of these, and you can interrupt the pattern of any emotion. Interrupt two of these, and the emotion will be totally annihilated. Do this regularly, and you will become a master at getting out of disempowering emotions and putting yourself into a productive state. PRIMARY FEARS Two primary fears are responsible for the emotional reactions that lead us into pain and destructive behaviors. We all have the fear that we're not enough, and that if we're not enough, we won't be loved. These primary fears are universal and never go away. Don't try to make them disappear— just be conscious and intelligent when they show up. Whenever you are upset, ask yourself "What beliefs am I holding on to that are making me feel that I'm not enough?"

DO A CHAIN OF CONSEQUENCES EXERCISE: This exercise will help you understand the beliefs that cause you pain. When you feel upset (stressed, fearful, angry, disappointed, etc.), what are you afraid is going to happen?

And if that were to happen, what would that mean?

And what would that mean?

To go behind this meaning and understand what's really going on, you must know the target we are all going after: the 6 Human Needs.

HUMAN NEEDS Everything we do, we do for six reasons only! The only difference between us is which needs we value most, and what we believe has to happen to meet those needs. Let's review these briefly

1. CERTAINTY Certainty that we can be comfortable—to have pleasure and to avoid pain. 2. UNCERTAINTY/VARIETY Variety and challenges which will exercise our emotional and physical range. 3. SIGNIFICANCE Every person needs to feel special, important, needed, wanted.

4. LOVE/CONNECTION Everyone needs connection with other human beings and everyone strives for and hopes for love. 5. GROWTH When we stop growing, we die. We need to constantly develop emotionally, intellectually, and spiritually. 6. CONTRIBUTION To go beyond your own needs and give to others. Everything in the universe contributes beyond itself or it is eliminated.

EXERCISE: What are your top two, driving needs?

How do you meet these:

In Positive Ways

In Negative Ways

What positive vehicles could you use to replace the negative ways?

If you have a partner, what are their top 2 Human Needs?

In what ways do they consistently meet those needs in a positive way?

In a negative way?

Everybody has variations in mood and attitude. Here is the pattern most people follow and why. In Tahnee's case, depression is way for her to connect and commiserate with herself. However, when this depression begins to make her feel too weak, she snaps out of it with anger. This emotional pattern of alternating between sadness and anger is called a crazy-eight. Many people live most of their lives alternating between these two emotions. We've all heard of "mood swings." The crazy-eight is a much more accurate description. Simply put, whatever your focus is and whatever emotions you experience, your body has to deal with them. And there are certain things your body can't deal with—for instance, if your predominant emotion is sadness, your body will not permit you to remain sad 100% of the time. It's a survival instinct—something deep in your physiology knows that if you stay sad, you will die, and so your body will work hard to give you relief from that sadness. For instance, at some point something inside Tahnee gets tired of being sad all of the time—at some point it feels weak, and so her focus snaps into anger, indignation, and defensiveness. With that as her focus, she will be tempted to find something to fight or someone to blame. This new energy may guide her to accomplish something at work and prove her worth. However, since this anger energy is not supported by feelings of connection and purpose, at some point it will lapse again into sadness. Hence, the crazy eight has gone full circle. The truth is that we all have crazy eights, because we all have the physiological need for emotional variety. The question is whether you allow your crazy eight to make your choices for you. For instance, you can anticipate your needs for emotional variety by giving yourself different things to focus on and do at different times.

EXERCISES: If you had a crazy eight emotional pattern, what would it be: (e.g. anger/helplessness, being controlling/withdrawing, trust/distrust)?

Tahnee's crazy eight revolved around the issue of trust—a relationship need she had not been able to create. If you had a crazy eight, what would be it's center? What is your crazy eight "about"?

Does your partner have a crazy eight? What is that about? What is your partner struggling with? What does he or she need?

TWO TYPES OF PROBLEMS QUALITY PROBLEMS involve a risky, forward-thinking decision that will often take you to another stage of progress in your life. Examples: career decisions, committing to a relationship, committing to a new standard in life. SAFE PROBLEMS are lingering, self-imposed feeling-states which come from a lack of sustainable ways to meet one's needs and a lack of vision for one's life. Examples: depression, addictions, blaming others, avoiding decisions, withdrawing from relationships. If you are getting upset without taking action, or if you are upset about factors that are out of your control (such as events in the past) then you are "maintaining" a safe problem. Take control of your ability to influence your own emotions. Make a shift in your physiology, your pattern of focus, and your language patterns. PROBLEMS ARE A SIGN OF LIFE! What are some problems that have been a regular challenge for you?

What is the risk associated with this problem? What if you succeed? What if you fail?

Does having this problem meet any of your 6 Human Needs? Which ones?

Is this a self-imposed "safe" problem, or a quality problem? If it's a "safe" problem, can you think of an underlying quality problem that it's related to?

What can you do about it?

Now consider your problem from this point of view. If you were to completely annihilate this "safe" problem from your life, how could you step up? How could you raise your standards? What would you do? How is this an opportunity to take your life and your relationship to a whole new level?

Everybody has primary emotional patterns that define their life—and will constrict their life, if they're not careful. Take a moment now to learn about your own patterns, and how to take steps to create the emotions you want to experience in life. FOR SINGLES: Do this exercise too! 1. Draw a line. On one side, write down the predominant empowering emotions you experience during the course of a week. On the other side, list your most common disempowering emotions. Circle the top two of each.

Disempowering Emotions

Empowering Emotions

How do your disempowering emotions meet your 6 Human Needs?

Where does this harm your life? What must you change?

What new emotion could you create as a new fuel of choice? What could you do with your body, focus, language, to embody this and create a new habit?

5

DAY 5: FROM SELFISH TO SELFLESSNESS: THE POWER OF UNCONDITIONAL LOVE

"Love the heart that hurts you, but never hurt the heart that loves you."
—Vipin Sharma

1. Heartfelt Understanding 2. Give Your Partner What They Really Need 3. Create and Build Trust and Respect 4. Reclaim Playfulness, Presence, and Passion 5. Harness Courage and Embrace Honesty 6. Uncover and Create Alignment 7. Live Consciously: Be An Example (Skill 7 applies to all 10 Disciplines of Love)

1. The Discipline of Putting Your Lover First: It's Not About You! 2. The Discipline of Loving No Matter What: The Power of Love, Adoration & Praise 3. The Discipline of Being Yourself: Emanate & Express Your Natural Essence & True Core 4. Discipline of Positive Intent: Eliminate Threats & Judgment & Remember The Power of Language 5. The Discipline of Freedom: The Power of Forgiving, Forgetting & Flooding 6. The Discipline of Daily Intimacy: Full Engagement—Open Your Heart & Hold Nothing Back 7. The Discipline of Polarity: The Power of Dancing Energies 8. The Discipline of Loving Truth: The Power of Vulnerability 9. The Discipline of Utilization: The Power of Higher Meaning & Constant Growth 10. The Discipline of Gratitude & Giving: Appreciation is the Power.

Today's session "From Selfish to Selflessness: The Liberating Power of Unconditional Love" will explore the second Master Relationship Skill: Giving Your Partner what They Really Need. Sometimes what matters most in relationship is not what you can do for your partner, but what you will do. Everything we do in relationship has natural consequences. In this session we will learn about the levels of giving and relationship and the natural consequences they create for you and your partner. The Discipline of the day is "Loving No Matter What." Often in relationship, we give only until we become uncomfortable, or something upsets or distracts us, and then we withdraw. That kind of giving can actually cause more damage. The truest gift comes from a long-term commitment, irrespective of short-term returns.

SCORE MARCUS AND BELLE ON THE 7 MASTER RELATIONSHIP SKILLS In this intervention, Cloé observed how Marcus and Belle rebuilt their relationship by building up their 7 Relationship Skills. What did you observe? Did you see the relationship skills being activated and leading to the next level of relationship? Let's start by scoring Marcus and Belle. Remember, this is your way to sharpen your powers of observation so that you can create progress in your relationship! SKILL 1: HEARTFELT UNDERSTANDING Marcus's Score:_____ What did Marcus understand or misunderstand about his wife's needs? Did he put her first?

"The essential conditions of everything you do must be choice, love, passion." —Nadia Boulanger

What did Marcus learn during the course of the conversation? How did that change him? How did that change her?

Belle's Score:_____ What did Belle understand or fail to understand about Marcus' needs? Where did that lead them?

What helped Belle to understand Marcus? Was it more information, or was it going into her heart?

SKILL 2: GIVE YOUR PARTNER WHAT THEY REALLY NEED Marcus's Score:_____ Which of Belle's needs was Marcus meeting? At what level was he meeting them? Why?

Was Marcus loving Belle no matter what? How did that affect their relationship?

Belle's Score:_____ Which of Marcus' needs did Belle meet or fail to meet? What was her motivation?

Was Belle loving Marcus no matter what, or not? What were her conditions?

SKILL 3: CREATE AND BUILD TRUST AND RESPECT Marcus's Score:_____ Had Marcus been building or destroying trust with Belle? What was his thinking?

What could Marcus have done to build trust? What did he learn during the conversation?

Belle's Score:_____ How was Belle thinking about Marcus' intentions towards her?

Did Belle give Marcus freedom, or guilt? What was fair or unfair about her behavior?

SKILL 4: RECLAIM PLAYFULNESS, PRESENCE, AND PASSION Marcus's Score:_____ Why weren't they enjoying daily intimacy? Did they have polarity?

What did Marcus learn about how to spark playfulness and passion?

Belle's Score:_____ Was Belle open to Marcus or not? What did she expect him to do? Was that reasonable?

What did Belle learn about playfulness? How did that serve their relationship?

SKILL 5: HARNESS COURAGE AND EMBRACE HONESTY Marcus's Score:_____ In the beginning, the couple was honest, at least about sexual matters. What happened? ______________________________

6

DAY 6: RELATIONSHIP STORMS: MAN ENOUGH TO STAY THE COURSE

SCORE SAMANTHA AND DARYL ON THE 7 MASTER RELATIONSHIP SKILLS Again, let's brush up on our observation of the 7 Master Relationship Skills by going through our checklist. What did you observe in Daryl and Samantha's conversation with Tony? What changed? When did you notice the shift? SKILL 1: HEARTFELT UNDERSTANDING Daryl's Score:_____ What did he learn? When did he get it?

"*1. Heartfelt Understanding 2. Give Your Partner What They Really Need 3. Create and Build Trust and Respect 4. Reclaim Playfulness, Presence, and Passion 5. Harness Courage and Embrace Honesty 6. Uncover and Create Alignment 7. Live Consciously: Be An Example (Skill 7 applies to all 10 Disciplines of Love)*"

"*1. The Discipline of Putting Your Lover First: It's Not About You! 2. The Discipline of Loving No Matter What: The Power of Love, Adoration & Praise 3. The Discipline of Being Yourself: Emanate & Express Your Natural Essence & True Core 4. Discipline of Positive Intent: Eliminate Threats & Judgment & Remember The Power of Language 5. The Discipline of Freedom: The Power of Forgiving, Forgetting & Flooding 6. The Discipline of Daily Intimacy: Full Engagement—Open Your Heart & Hold Nothing Back 7. The Discipline of Polarity: The Power of Dancing Energies 8. The Discipline of Loving Truth: The Power of Vulnerability 9. The Discipline of Utilization: The Power of Higher Meaning & Constant Growth 10. The Discipline of Gratitude & Giving: Appreciation is the Power"*

SKILL 1: HEARTFELT UNDERSTANDING Daryl's Score:_____ What did he learn? When did he get it?

Did you see a good example of this skill?

"Let me be my last word, that I trust in your love." —Rabindranath Tagore

Samantha's Score:_____ What was her greatest challenge with this skill?

What had she not understood about Daryl?

SKILL 2: GIVE YOUR PARTNER WHAT THEY REALLY NEED Daryl's Score:_____ What did he learn?

Samantha's Score:_____ What did Samantha have to overcome to practice this skill?

What did she learn?

SKILL 3: CREATE AND BUILD TRUST AND RESPECT Daryl's Score:_____ What had Daryl been doing that failed to build trust and respect in his relationship?

Did you see a good example of this skill?

What did he learn to do that day?

Samantha's Score:_____ What was her greatest challenge with this skill?

Samantha's Score:_____ What was preventing Samantha from being playful?

When did this turn around for her?

What did she learn?

SKILL 4: RECLAIM PLAYFULNESS, PRESENCE, AND PASSION Daryl's Score:_____ How much of this skill was Daryl displaying at first?

SKILL 5: HARNESS COURAGE AND EMBRACE HONESTY Daryl's Score:_____ What did Daryl need to communicate in order to be honest?

Was there a moment where his ability turned around?

When did this turn around?

Samantha's Score:_____ How did Samantha lack courage and honesty in the beginning?

Samantha's Score:_____ At the beginning, did Samantha feel aligned with Daryl? Why?

What did she learn?

What did she learn?

SKILL 6: UNCOVER AND CREATE ALIGNMENT Daryl's Score:_____ At the beginning, had Daryl created alignment?

SKILL 7: LIVE CONSCIOUSLY: BE AN EXAMPLE Daryl's Score:_____ What kind of example was Daryl setting for his children?

What did Daryl do to create alignment?

How did Samantha feel about this?

Samantha's Score:_____ What kind of example was Samantha setting?

What would have been the consequences of this example for her children?

Do you know any couples or individuals like Samantha and Daryl? What did you learn from Samantha and Daryl's example?

Out of the Mouths of Babes

"No person really decides before they grow up who they're going to marry. God decides it all way before, and you get to find out later who you're stuck with." —Kirsten, age 10

WHAT DID YOU LEARN? POINTS TO REMEMBER: THE ART OF BUILDING AND REBUILDING TRUST The challenge is that trust is formed not during easy times, but in defining moments of difficulty and stress, when our loyalties, our priorities, and our commitment come into question. That is why creating trust is about how to face our deepest fears, tap into our inner strength, and bring to our partners what they need most. When you can build trust in times of difficulty and stress, the relationship will grow and flourish. When during those moments you fail to increase your trust, you will have difficulty making progress in many areas of your relationship. The principle behind trust is quite simple. We trust people when we feel they care about what we need. Trust is built at those moments when the pressure is such that you are tempted to put yourself first and put your partner's needs second. That is precisely the time to take the opportunity to put your partner first and so create a strong bond of trust and love. Trust is based on mutual high standards about meeting each other's needs. When you and your partner are confidently and firmly devoted to a level three relationship, all heck can break loose yet you know that you won't get left behind. If your mutual standards are level two, then you know you can trust your partner as far as their needs are being met. At some point, however, your partner may say, "Look, this is unreasonable. I have to meet this need, and you must be responsible for your needs as well." At that point the relationship has dropped to a level one, where in an environment of scarcity, the two partners end up competing for whose needs get met and who is going to go without. Sound familiar? Ever heard of any divorces that took this route? Most of us have.

THE FIVE STAGES OF BUILDING TRUST Trust is depleted when partners lose their commitment to each other, let go of the other's needs, and put their own individual needs first. In the same way, trust can be rebuilt by proving your commitment to your partner over time and during periods of tests. Since trust is built by testing it, you can accelerate trust in your relationship by following the five stages of building trust in difficult circumstances.

- Commit and Declare
- Create Heartfelt Emotion
- Share, Listen, Learn
- Align Vision Love
- Act of love

STAGE ONE:

"COMMIT AND DECLARE. The basis of trust is your commitment to put your partner's needs first. You cannot build trust when you are focusing on yourself and putting yourself first. You cannot say that you will create trust once you've gotten what you want. You must start by declaring your absolute commitment to your partner. For instance, you can say: "I love you too much to argue with you." "I love you and I will take care of you no matter what."

STAGE TWO:

"CREATE HEARTFELT EMOTION that will bring healing and love. Breathe deeply, put your hand on your heart, look into your partner's eyes and express your love. Go back into yourself, close your eyes, breathe deeply. Connect from your hear to his or her heart. Feel the love that binds you. Stay in your heart until all negative emotions are outweighed by your gratitude and love. Do not proceed to stage three

until you have heartfelt emotion for your partner. "

STAGE THREE: SHARE, LISTEN, LEARN. Tell the truth about your feelings and listen to your partner without trying to fix or resolve anything. Your partner may express doubt, hesitation, regret or disappointment. When this happens, show your loving determination to put your partner first and to honor his or her need for love. Don't see your partner's feedback as an attack—see it as a request for more love from you. Whatever your partner says, give him or her a loving response.

STAGE FOUR: ALIGN AND CREATE VISION. Align with your partner and create a compelling future. Hear your partner's requests, learn about your partner's needs, and think of ways to meet these underlying needs. Give him or her a loving response. Repeat your declaration of love and commitment. Think of ways to create a common vision of the future, combining your needs and your partner's needs. STAGE FIVE: ACT OF LOVE. Always end difficult conversations with an act of love: a kiss, a hug, a reference to a happy memory, a promise. If you cannot end with an act of love, then you have not succeeded in building trust. Go back to stages one through four. Remember, trust is either won or lost, there is no third option. Trust is built by repeating and reinforcing these five levels: from commitment, to generating loving emotions, to sharing and listening, to giving a loving response, to aligning for a compelling future, to acts of love. The next time you find yourself in a difficult conversation with your partner, take a moment to understand which stage the conversation is at. Is your partner feeling your love, understanding, and commitment? Do you have heartfelt emotion towards your partner? Is it safe for your partner to share his or her experience, while you listen? Are you capable of giving a loving response, no matter what your partner's emotional state is? Once you and your partner have shared and communicated, align and create a shared vision, so that when you are back together, the exercise is sealed by an act of love.

PRESENCE EXERCISE There is a specific exercise for creating trust on an emotional level in stressful times—this is the exercise Tony did with Samantha and Daryl. There are two separate roles, for men and for women. Presence Exercise for Men: Look into her eyes. Go to what she's thinking about. Share her emotions. Go to her feelings even if they are negative and opposing you. Don't try to change her, just be with her. While staying physically solid and still, imagine going into her body and feel what she's feeling, experience what she's experiencing. Use any clues to figure out how she's feeling, without judgment or distraction. Don't posture or position, don't worry about what you look like. Just focus your total attention on feeling and understanding her.

REALITY CHECK: Presence doesn't necessarily mean staring silently into your partner. You must know how your partner communicates. If he or she is biased towards auditory communication, communicate your commitment verbally. If they are visual, present visually to him or her, watching for their response. If your partner is touch-based, your job is easy—caress and hold. Heart Exercise for Women: Go to your heart and let it open to him. Feel his full presence. If he seems distracted, scared or stuck in thought, give him a slap on the shoulder. The purpose is not to hurt him but to give him direct feedback, to help him to be fully engaged, bring him to full attention. Slap him to wake him up, give him the feedback he needs. Help him to be present for you. This is the greatest gift you can give him. When you feel his full presence reward him with a hug and a kiss. REALITY CHECK: Be true to your feelings, but don't hold out either! This is a fine line, and a time to be connected by your heart. If you can feel your partner's earnest effort, his confidence, and his devotion, encourage him.

"DO IT NOW: DAY 6 ASSIGNMENT Today focuses on one of the most crucial skills for restoring trust during times of conflict. As we know, the first two Master Relationship Skills are Heartfelt Understanding and Giving to Your Partner. This heart breathing exercise will naturally put you into your natural emotional center, where heartfelt understanding is effortless. From that state, you can make more heartfelt and integrated decisions for your life and your relationship. 1. Think of something that has been upsetting you. Something that bothers you enough to make a physiological impact on you. 2. Breathe into your heart, feel its power and intelligence. Don't think—return your attention to your heart—for 2 minutes. 3. When finished, ask your heart what you need to know. Accept the first answer. 4. Go to your partner, give them something, and make a commitment to them."

7

DAY 7: THE POWER OF CONNECTION: REKINDLING INTIMACY WITH YOUR LOVER

In today's session, "The Power of Connection: Rekindling Intimacy with Your Lover," we will explore the fourth Master Relationship Skill of Reclaiming Playfulness, Presence, and Passion. Once you have a basis of Heartfelt Understanding, Giving, and Trust, the next leap is to dive into passionate intimacy. For this, the essential disciplines are The Discipline of Full Engagement: Open Your Heart and Hold Nothing Back and The Discipline of Polarity: The Power of Dancing Energies.

THE 7 MASTER RELATIONSHIP SKILLS SCORE CARD: SCORE ARONTZA AND ALAN Often we think that we are giving our partner what is most important and what they really want and are surprised to find that our love is not received in the way that we intended. If you watched or listened to Arontza and Alan you know that Arontza expressed with no uncertainty that she was not getting the kind of love and attention that she needed from her husband, even though her husband was a loving and caring man. Even the way Alan hugged and kissed Arontza did not meet her needs for feeling loved. Sharpen your powers of observation and understanding of full engagement, intimacy, and presence by scoring Alan and Arontza.

SKILL 1: HEARTFELT UNDERSTANDING Alan's Score:_____ What stood in the way of showing heartfelt understanding for his wife?

"It is only with the heart that one sees rightly; what is essential is invisible to the eye." —St. Antoine d' Exupéry

What did he learn?

Arontza's Score:_____ What did she understand about her husband? What didn't she?

What did she learn?

Arontza's Score:_____ Which needs did Arontza satisfy for Alan? Which did she not fulfill?

What did she learn?

SKILL 3: CREATE AND BUILD TRUST AND RESPECT Alan's Score:_____ How aware was Alan about the necessity of building trust?

What did he learn?

Arontza's Score:_____ What did Arontza trust/respect about Alan? What did she not trust/respect?

How did that affect the relationship? What did she learn?

Arontza's Score:_____ Was Arontza ready for Alan's presence?

What was her greatest challenge?

SKILL 4: RECLAIM PLAYFULNESS, PRESENCE, AND PASSION Alan's Score:_____ Where did or didn't Alan show his presence? What stood in his way?

What was her greatest challenge?

What did she learn?

SKILL 5: HARNESS COURAGE AND EMBRACE HONESTY Alan's Score:_____ Why?

What did he learn?

Arontza's Score:_____ Why?

What was her greatest challenge?

What was her greatest challenge? What did she learn?

SKILL 6: UNCOVER AND CREATE ALIGNMENT Alan's Score:_____ Where did you see alignment or lack of alignment?

SKILL 7: LIVE CONSCIOUSLY: BE AN EXAMPLE Alan's Score:_____ Imagine: What kind of examples was Alan following from his own life?

Do you know any couples or individuals like Arontza and Alan? What did you learn from their example?

Notes

What did he learn?

Arontza's Score:_____ Imagine: What kind of examples was Arontza following from her life?

What did she learn?

Out of the Mouths of Babes "Dates are for having fun, and people should use them to get to know each other. Even boys have something to say if you listen long enough." —Lynnette, age 8

SIX STEPS FOR RENEWING INTIMACY WITH YOUR LOVER Intimacy is about letting your partner under your skin— physically and emotionally. It's an opening and a vulnerability which must be earned, not taken for granted, and once you have intimacy, it must be appreciated, cherished, and cultivated. In order to initiate intimacy, especially after a period of distance between you and your partner, it helps to follow these six steps for orienting you and learning what your partner needs. STEP ONE: SPECIFY WHAT, WHEN AND HOW Most people have a perceptual bias in how they experience the world. Is your partner more receptive to visual, auditory, or kinesthetic or touch stimulus? Once you know this, you can be much more conscious and effective in how you communicate and give to your partner. If your partner is primarily and auditory person, keyed in to language, tonality, and rhythm, then they may not understand what you mean when you stare lovingly into their face. On the other hand, we all know people who do not get what you're telling them until you show them visually, or show them by getting them to do something themselves. If you can discover your partner's perceptual bias—whether they are most sensitive to the visual, the auditory, or the kinesthetic (bodily sensation)—you will discover the key to stimulating intimacy in them. Do you know how your partner responds to communication best? Watch him or her respond to different cues during the course of the day. Is your partner's primary modality visual, auditory or kinesthetic?

Does your partner respond best to your facial expression, your voice or your touch?

Rank these three types in order of effectiveness in your partner: Visual ________ Auditory________ Kinesthetic ________ Are combinations effective for your partner? Do they need to be told something while being touched? Or do they need to see your face as well as hear you?

Which modality do you favor: visual, auditory or kinesthetic?

Think of a time when your partner felt loved by you. Which modality were you communicating in? Which modality does he or she favor?

Although we all have the same 6 Human Needs, we value them in different proportion. Step two is to learn which your partner's top two needs are and what has to happen for them to experience those needs. Here again are the 6 Human Needs:

"1. CERTAINTY Certainty that we can be comfortable—to have pleasure and to avoid pain. 2. UNCERTAINTY/VARIETY Variety and challenges which will exercise our emotional and physical range. 3. SIGNIFICANCE Every person needs to feel special, important, needed, wanted."

"4. LOVE/CONNECTION Everyone needs connection with other human beings and everyone strives for and hopes for love. 5. GROWTH When we stop growing, we die. We need to constantly develop emotionally, intellectually, and spiritually. 6. CONTRIBUTION To go beyond your own needs and give to others. Everything in the universe contributes beyond itself or it is eliminated."

Which of these needs does your partner value most? Which need comes in second place?

What has to happen for your partner to feel that his or her needs are being met?

Can you think of some other, more surprising ways for meeting those needs? Be creative—think of three or more ways to meet your partner's top two needs.

STEP THREE: WHO GOES FIRST? When neither spouse wants to be first in initiating love, then intimacy cannot flow free. However, most men and most women have a preference—even a fantasy—of how the affection should flow. What is your fantasy? What is your partner's fantasy? Who should initiate?

Polarity is powered by the attraction of opposites. If both partners are hanging back and waiting, there can be no polarity, because they are imitating each other. How can you create more polarity with your partner?

What does your partner have to do to let you know he or she really desires you? Be precise: write down exact actions, looks or words.

STEP FOUR: COMMIT If you are weighing alternatives to your relationship you are not committed, meaning that your relationship is dying, not growing. Passion comes from an element of uncertainty and even discomfort. If you want to experience the fullness of passion, you need to step out of your comfort zones and take some risks. Which risks have you been avoiding in your relationship.

Heart Meditation: This meditation puts you in touch with your heartfelt inner strength. Whenever you feel overwhelmed with feelings and thoughts, this simple meditation can cut through complications and anxieties and remind you of what matters most to you. Breathe into your heart and feel its power. Think of a moment in your life when you felt deeply connected and grateful for your partner, for his or her love. Breathe deeply and close your eyes. Keep other thoughts away. Feel your heart beating and breathe into your heart. Think of a time when you felt really connected and grateful for your partner. Think of a second time when you felt really grateful for having your partner. Think of another time when you felt grateful for your partner and when you felt loved by him/her. Breathe deeply into your heart and think of another time you felt connected, maybe a sexy moment. Ask yourself in this state: What do I need to do to reach in and feel and connect with my partner, to have him/her feel my inner strength and my inner love? Now open your eyes and do whatever is natural.

Ask Yourself: Why are you grateful for your partner?

When do you feel deeply connected to your partner?

How can you increase the frequency and intensity of those times when you feel deeply connected to your partner?

How can you strengthen your commitment to your relationship?

STEP FIVE: EXPERIMENT You need to experiment with many ways of giving. Watch to see which things your lover enjoys most, and give him or her more of that. Be creative. One of the beauties of the 6 Human Needs is that there are many ways of meeting them. Remember what you wrote in Step One about how your partner communicates best. What are some new ways that you could show your partner that you love her/him?

1.

2.

3.

4.

5.

6.

7.

Don't be discouraged if some of them don't work. This is a process of elimination! Keep note of how your partner responds and learn from it. Are there some activities or special things from your early dating period that you can reintroduce into your relationship that will increase intimacy?

STEP SIX: OPEN UP Intimacy is a matter of the heart—don't expect to succeed unless you are willing to feel your connection with your partner. Relax, breathe into your heart and enjoy whatever happens. Have either you or your partner created barriers to intimacy? If so, what can you do to remove the barriers?

What can you do to open yourself to more intimacy?

How can you help your partner to become more open to intimacy and passion?

DO IT NOW: DAY 7 ASSIGNMENT PRACTICE POLARITY One partner takes on the masculine position and the other the feminine. The masculine pays intense attention to the feminine as they both stand looking into each other's eyes. The feminine pays attention to her feelings to see if and when she/he is moved by the masculine presence. When the feminine feels the other's presence she will be moved and respond spontaneously. The feminine may test the strength and dedication of the masculine and the masculine must stay the course without recoiling or withdrawing. During this practice, cultivate the moments of success and learn what works for your partner. Focus on Love and on the yearning to understand and to feel what is going on inside your partner. Don't focus on your own needs. Remember that your partner is who he/she is and you cannot change your partner, you can only change yourself. For Men Only: give your woman your presence. Get rooted in your life purpose and what you want to deliver to your woman. For Women: open up to your man's efforts—don't fake, don't block them. Be aware and open.

"Passion begins where your bodies unite and ends where your souls dance. When your spirits can join together at the same time as your bodies become one, then all of you will be making love. There will be nothing left between you that is not love. This is sacred communion. This is ecstasy."
—Barbara D'Angelis

8

DAY 8: TAKING OFF YOUR MASK: THE POWER OF LIGHT AND DARK

Here again we explore the fourth Master Relationship Skill of Reclaiming Playfulness, Presence, and Passion. A crucial part of relationship lies in your ability to influence your partner's feelings and needs. Being playful, present, and passionate—and practicing the Discipline of Polarity—are ways to get into your partner and stimulate the passionate play that relationship is all about.

SCORE JUSTIN AND RUTH ON THE 7 MASTER RELATIONSHIP SKILLS Take a moment to sharpen your observation and understanding of Justin and Ruth's progress during their conversation with Tony. When initiating intimacy and passionate love in your own relationships, everybody encounters obstacles and moments of uncertainty. The better you are at understanding how human needs are met and how relationship skills are strengthened, the greater results you'll have in your own relationship.

SKILL 1: HEARTFELT UNDERSTANDING Justin's Score:_____ How did Justin understand his wife? What did he not understand?

What changed?

"Love is the answer, but while you are waiting for the answer, sex raises some pretty good questions." —Woody Allen

Ruth's Score:_____ What was Ruth's attitude towards Justin at first?

Ruth's Score:_____ Which of Justin's needs was Ruth meeting? Which were not being met?

What happened during the course of the conversation?

SKILL 2: GIVE YOUR PARTNER WHAT THEY REALLY NEED Justin's Score:_____ Which of Ruth's needs was Justin meeting? Which were not being met?

What did she learn?

SKILL 3: CREATE AND BUILD TRUST AND RESPECT Justin's Score:_____ Was Justin practicing the discipline of being himself?

Which needs in particular did he learn to meet in her?

What did he learn to do?

Ruth's Score:_____ What did Ruth trust in Justin? Was that enough?

What did she have to overcome in order to experience trust?

SKILL 4: RECLAIM PLAYFULNESS, PRESENCE, AND PASSION Justin's Score:_____ What prevented Justin from being present, passionate, and playful?

Ruth's Score:_____ What did Ruth need in order to become playful?

What was the turning point in her ability to experience passion?

SKILL 5: HARNESS COURAGE AND EMBRACE HONESTY Justin's Score:_____ What kind of courage did Justin need?

What did he learn was necessary for passion? What was not necessary?

What did he learn?

Ruth's Score:_____ Where did Ruth need courage?

What was her turning point?

SKILL 6: UNCOVER AND CREATE ALIGNMENT Justin's Score:_____ What kind of alignment did this couple have at first?

Ruth's Score:_____ What did Ruth have to do for alignment to take place?

Do you believe that this couple is aligned now?

SKILL 7: LIVE CONSCIOUSLY: BE AN EXAMPLE Justin's Score:_____ Imagine: what kinds of examples had been guiding Justin?

How did Justin find alignment with Ruth?

What kind of example does he need to create?

Ruth's Score:_____ What kind of examples do you think Ruth had?

What will it take for their new example to flourish?

Do you know any individuals or couples like Justin and Ruth?

What did you learn from Justin and Ruth's example?

WHAT DID YOU LEARN? POINTS TO REMEMBER THE ROLES WE PLAY Some of the greatest relationship limitations come from the feeling that we need to behave in certain, restricted ways. For many couples there is such a sense of decorum and consideration, that this blocks the assertive, familiarity that makes intimacy possible. Today we want to work on the ways that we break through these restrictions and express ourselves in a heartfelt, passionate way. Are there things that you don't say or do for fear of being criticized?

Are there lines that you don't cross with your partner? How do you hold back?

What happens as a result of holding back? What are you not sharing?

What would you share or give if you knew it was absolutely safe?

Are you willing to keep your focus and connection with your partner even when you are criticized?

IMPLICIT AND EXPLICIT COMMUNICATION Men tend to communicate explicitly—saying factually what they want and what they mean. Women tend to communicate implicitly—with more awareness of the subtler emotional and interactive dynamics. In most traditional cultures, it is the man's job to initiate—to pursue the woman romantically. Many women still expect that the man will have the direction, the resolve and the desire to initiate. What confuses men most is when women make an implicit suggestion (that he initiate, that he do something for her, that he take charge) and then seem to change their mind. This is "testing" —testing to see whether the man will follow through with his initiative. When the feminine partner is testing her masculine partner, she is asking, testing, wondering, checking, reassuring herself, that he desires her and that he will follow through no matter what. Let's practice implicit and explicit communication. Imagine That you're driving with your partner and one of you would like to stop and get an ice cream. An explicit way of communicating that would be "Hey, can we stop there for a second? I really feel like an ice cream."

A more implicit way of asking for ice cream would be "Wouldn't some ice cream taste good right now?" And an even more implicit way of saying that would be "Do you like ice cream?" or "Would you like some ice cream?" Very typically, one partner fails to understand the other partner's implicit communication, leading to frustration and confusion. How would you have responded to these questions? Would you have known that your partner was actually asking you to pull over? FOR SINGLES: Answer these questions in relation to a former relationship.

Are there times in your relationship where you may not be understanding your partner's implicit requests? Are your requests being understood?

How can you be more sensitive to each other's communication styles? How could you be more clear with a masculine listener? How could you be more sensitive and proactive with a feminine listener?

EXPAND YOUR IDENTITY: LIGHT AND DARK Everyone has an emotional spectrum that runs from "light" emotions of loyalty, understanding and service to "dark" emotions of sexual desire, naughtiness and sexual possession. When partners restrict their range of emotional expression they restrict their passion.

EXERCISE: FIND YOUR PARTNER'S FORBIDDEN NAME Often what we look for in passionate intimacy is a complete vacation from our everyday life. Intimacy is a great way to relax from typical roles and responsibilities and to experience uncertainty, excitement, and spontaneity. In the audio session, Ruth needed to get away from the burden of being so responsible for everything and everybody. What Justin needed was a way of breaking her pattern of stress and responsibility, sweeping her off of her feet, and taking her into passionate exchange. To this purpose, Tony helped Justin and Ruth to discover her "forbidden name." This is a name which Ruth would never admit to herself was sexy, crazy, and attractive. It seemed like the last thing she wanted or needed, but "Roxy" was there, right below the surface. Now, ask yourself: does your lover have nicknames that you may not have discovered yet?

How could you make use of your lover's nicknames to create a feeling of love and playfulness?

What activities, thoughts and fantasies can you indulge in to bring out your feminine/your masculine?

In your relationship, do you cultivate a safe place with your partner where you can get away from your responsibilities?

Do you and your partner have rituals where you connect and love each other?

Do you know what to do to make your partner feel cherished and taken care of?

"For men, what can you do to take charge of the situation so your woman can relax and simply enjoy your initiative in loving her?"

"For women, what can you do to relax and open emotionally so that your man can enjoy your happiness and emotion?"

"Create a ritual that you will practice once a day and a ritual that you will practice once a week where both of you can relax and enjoy intimacy. It may be physical intimacy or it may be a cup of tea, a few extra minutes in bed talking, or a walk. What will you commit to do with each other?"

"Out of the Mouths of Babes When is it okay to kiss someone? "The law says you have to be eighteen, so I wouldn't want to mess with that." —Curt, age 7"

1. What rules are getting in the way of your relationship? What are your rules about how to be? The worst difficulty is when one person in the relationship takes on a new role (mother, father, husband, wife) and imposes that on the relationship. Don't unconsciously impose old rules and beliefs onto your relationship. What rule needs to be taken out of your relationship—about sensuality, what's bad, what's appropriate?

2. What's a belief that you need to bring into the relationship— an identity, a role, an emotion. What's one for you?

3. What's an identity, or two or three, for you to play with, and play with each other. To open each other up more.

4. If you're the man, what are you going to do to initiate? How are you going to light up your partner in ways that may surprise them? How could you stimulate your partner's dark side?

Notes

Notes

9

DAY 9: FINDING YOUR TRUE PASSION: THE POWER OF HONESTY IN ACTION

"In a time of universal deceit, telling the truth becomes a revolutionary act."
—George Orwell

"1. Heartfelt Understanding 2. Give Your Partner What They Really Need 3. Create and Build Trust and Respect 4. Reclaim Playfulness, Presence, and Passion 5. Harness Courage and Embrace Honesty 6. Uncover and Create Alignment 7. Live Consciously: Be An Example (Skill 7 applies to all 10 Disciplines of Love) The 7 Master Skills The 10 Disciplines of Love 1. The Discipline of Putting Your Lover First: It's Not About You! 2. The Discipline of Loving No Matter What: The Power of Love, Adoration & Praise 3. The Discipline of Being Yourself: Emanate & Express Your Natural Essence & True Core 4. Discipline of Positive Intent: Eliminate Threats & Judgment & Remember The Power of Language 5. The Discipline of Freedom: The Power of Forgiving, Forgetting & Flooding 6. The Discipline of Daily Intimacy: Full Engagement—Open Your Heart & Hold Nothing Back 7. The Discipline of Polarity: The Power of Dancing Energies 8. The Discipline of Loving Truth: The Power of Vulnerability 9. The Discipline of Utilization: The Power of Higher Meaning & Constant Growth 10. The

Discipline of Gratitude & Giving: Appreciation is the Power "

We will explore the fifth Master Relationship Skill of Harnessing Courage and Embracing Honesty. At any point in your relationship— and even when you're in a great state—it is important to practice honesty and courage in the moment. This means communicating your feelings without either suppressing the truth or offending your partner. If you don't do this, suppressed emotion will build up and explode. The Discipline for today is the Discipline of Loving Truth: The Power of Vulnerability.

SCORE KAREN AND WARREN ON THE 7 MASTER RELATIONSHIP SKILLS Take a moment to sharpen your skills of observation. Remember, this is the way to master the 7 Relationship Skills—observe their strengths and weaknesses, and what consequences these bring. High standards in life and in relationship comes from being fully aware of the consequences of having low standards. SKILL 1: HEARTFELT UNDERSTANDING Warren's Score:_____ What did he understand? What didn't he understand?

What did he learn?

"Where there is love, there is life." —Mahatma Gandhi

Karen's Score:_____ What did she understand or fail to understand?

Karen's Score:_____ Which of Warren's needs was she meeting? Which wasn't she meeting?

What did she learn?

SKILL 2: GIVE YOUR PARTNER WHAT THEY REALLY NEED Warren's Score:_____ Which of Karen's needs was Warren meeting? Which wasn't he meeting?

What did he learn?

Karen's Score:_____ Which of Warren's needs was she meeting? Which wasn't she meeting?

What did she learn?

SKILL 3: CREATE AND BUILD TRUST AND RESPECT Warren's Score:_____ What did Warren trust or mistrust in Karen? In himself?

Karen's Score:_____ What Karen feel certain about? Positive or negative?

What did she learn?

Karen's Score:_____ Did Karen know she needed playfulness, presence, and passion? Why?

What did she learn?

SKILL 4: RECLAIM PLAYFULNESS, PRESENCE, AND PASSION Warren's Score:_____ What happened when Warren became present?

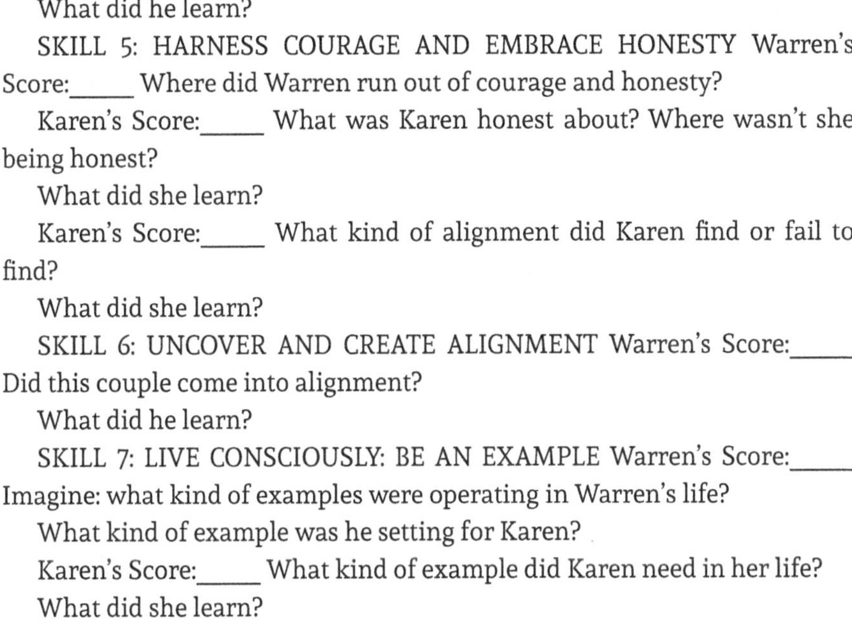

What did he learn?

SKILL 5: HARNESS COURAGE AND EMBRACE HONESTY Warren's Score:_____ Where did Warren run out of courage and honesty?

Karen's Score:_____ What was Karen honest about? Where wasn't she being honest?

What did she learn?

Karen's Score:_____ What kind of alignment did Karen find or fail to find?

What did she learn?

SKILL 6: UNCOVER AND CREATE ALIGNMENT Warren's Score:_____ Did this couple come into alignment?

What did he learn?

SKILL 7: LIVE CONSCIOUSLY: BE AN EXAMPLE Warren's Score:_____ Imagine: what kind of examples were operating in Warren's life?

What kind of example was he setting for Karen?

Karen's Score:_____ What kind of example did Karen need in her life?

What did she learn?

Do you know any individuals or couples like Karen and Warren? What did you learn from Karen and Warren's example?

WHAT DID YOU LEARN? POINTS TO REMEMBER When partners have trouble getting to clear, effective communication, it is likely that they are stumbling into a "double-bind" that is blocking their ability to make the relationship thrive.

A double-bind is the simultaneous communication of two incongruous injunctions within the context of an intense relationship. You must take action, but you are given mixed messages on how to act and you feel that you are "damned if you do, damned if you don't." This is one of the main reasons why people don't take action.

> "*Let's look at some examples: Someone tells you to "be spontaneous." This is a paradox—they are directing you to act on your own accord but it is impossible to fulfill the command without violating it as well. If you say or do something in response to the person's command, you are not being spontaneous—you are merely reacting to the order. On the other hand, if you do nothing, you are also not being spontaneous. A wife wants her husband to make more money, but she hates it when he stays at work late. If working late is necessary to making more money, then he doesn't feel that he can win. The double-bind is not an*

abstract concept. It is one of the most common triggers we have for feelings of helplessness and frustration at not being able to take action. In fact, you could say that "where there is inaction, there is a double-bind"—there is a failure to get rewarded for taking a course of action."

The Structure of Injunctions in Straightforward Communication: Successful, straightforward communication follows a certain order. Step One: A request is made, i.e. "Bring me a glass of water." Step Two: The request is fulfilled, i.e. I bring you a glass of water. Step Three: Fulfillment of the request is acknowledged, i.e. "Thank you." The Structure of Injunctions in Double-Bind Communication: Double-bind communication interrupts straightforward communication and prevents a successful outcome. Step One: A request is made, i.e. "Come give me a hug." Step Two: The request is fulfilled, i.e. I come over and hug you. Step Three:Fulfillment of the request is prevented, i.e. as I hug you, you push me away.

STEP ONE: UNDERSTAND THE TWO CONTRADICTORY MESSAGES AND THEIR CONSEQUENCES Double-binding communication is, in fact, very common in every day life. Here are some questions to guide you to uncover confusion and uncertainty and to decide on how to respond to double-binds. FOR SINGLES: Answer these questions in relation to a former relationship. Are there any areas of your life where there is inaction or a major problem?

Have you put yourself in a double-bind situation? Be aware that you probably have double-binds in a number of your relationships—at home, at work, with a friend. Think of one relationship where there has been a failure to take decisive action, can you see a double-bind there? What double-bind messages do you get in your love relationship?

The first message in a double-bind situation is the direct command that is spoken out loud. What, in your case, was the first message?

Out of the Mouths of Babes What do most people do on a date? "On the first date, they just tell each other lies, and that usually gets them interested enough to go for a second date." —Martin, age 10

The second message in a double-bind is the incongruent or opposite message. Often times this is the "hidden" message. What was your second message?

What will happen if you continue to be double bound in that way? Are you willing to continue to live with those consequences?

What do you do when you feel double bound? Which message do you respond to?

What do you feel would happen if you failed to respond to one of the messages? What would be the actual consequences?

Now think of a relationship in your life where you are the senior member (at work, with your children, with your siblings). Can you think of a time when you may have "set" a doublebind? Did you ask for something that you did not permit to happen? Did you ask for something that you did not reward or acknowledge?

STEP TWO: TAKE RESPONSIBILITY FOR YOUR OWN POWER What does it mean to take responsibility for your own power? Does it mean that you beat yourself up with guilt about what you did or didn't do in the past? Does it mean that you "positive think" yourself until you become powerful in real life? Simply put, taking responsibility means that you are deciding to value the solution over the problem. You can continue to feel that you're "damned if you do and damned if you don't" or you can simply decide to get out of your dilemma and find another way. Think of the consequences of the double-binds in your life. Were you really double bound, or did you double bound yourself? Look back and be honest. Don't beat yourself up; just be honest.

What was the impact on that relationship?

How could you make your communication and your desires more clear? Remember, double-binds occur out of a lack of clarity. Specifically, double-binds occur from wanting someone to do something specific, but to do it of their own accord. Can you think of a way that you may have ordered someone to do something "of their own accord?"

What actually happened? How effective was your communication? Did you get what you wanted?

How can you be more clear about your desires? How could you be more careful about rewarding this person for their efforts?

STEP THREE: RECOGNIZE THE INTERNAL CONFLICTS THAT LED TO THE DOUBLE-BIND The secret to overcoming a double-bind in a relationship is to recognize your partner's needs and to focus on meeting them. Look beneath the surface and see what your partner's true needs are. Double-binds within relationships come from a mixture of desire and fear. If you can understand your partner's needs and fears, you can instantly resolve the double-bind. If someone in your life is giving you mixed or contradictory messages, instead of getting confused, try understanding which needs they are trying to meet (certainty, uncertainty/ variety, significance, love, growth, contribution). Think of new ways that you can meet your partner's needs. The doublebind communication is a wake-up call to understand and respond to your partner's needs. Which of your partner's needs are not being met? Remember, if you can understand your partner's needs, you can resolve the double-bind immediately. What are your partner's rules for meeting this need?

How can you meet your partner's needs in new and surprising ways?

Most double-binds come from a conflict between the need for stimulus and the need to feel safe. How can you provide both?

How are you going to reconcile the two sets of needs? How are you going to make sure that both you and your partner get your needs met?

STEP FOUR: CLARIFY WHO YOU REALLY ARE A thriving, passionate relationship is rarely based on obedience and conformity to the other's wishes. Romance requires more initiative. Relationships that are fully alive will usually have the partners looking deeply into each other's needs, finding surprising and passionate ways to serve and even challenge each other. When the partners disagree, they speak their mind with passion! That is the route to passionate honesty and intimacy. So here's the bottom line about double-binds: double-binds come from trying to "obey" the person "setting" the doublebind. You can be double bound as a child by your parents or as an adult by your boss or by your superior in a hierarchical organization such as the military. However, if you are double bound in your romantic relationship, you need to make a quantum shift in your thinking. You will not get the relationship you want from "obeying" your partner like a child—especially if you do not necessarily agree with your partner's demands. Of course, a relationship is a two-way street and does require compromise, negotiation, discussion, and giving to the other even when you don't fully understand. These are different from blind obedience. If you care about your partner, ask them what's really going on! Figure it out! What are you willing to do in order to meet your partner's deepest needs?

STEP FIVE: DEMONSTRATE YOUR RESPONSIBILITY, PASSION, AND INITIATIVE As we have seen over and over, intellectual knowledge will only get you so far. You could go through the first three steps of overcoming a double-bind—understanding, taking responsibility and clarifying—but this will not help you unless you implement what you know in a strong way. Especially if you have been habitually double bound for more than a few days, you will need to take strong action to regain your freedom, your emotional muscle, and your partner's greater happiness. What kind of action can you take to show your partner what you're made of?

What does your partner care about? What does your partner need?

Step five is about making absolutely sure that you act on what you know. If you or your partner have been double bound for a long time, it is going to feel unfamiliar to be proactive and free. If you are accustomed to being stuck and conforming to dilemmas, it may seem difficult to skip over the usual ineffective dilemmas and go straight for your partner's needs. The main lesson here is to observe your partner closely for what they like and what they need and then to just decide to give them what they need. Take note of your partner's needs. Discover not only which of the 6 Needs they favor most but also what their rules are for having their needs met. Some people only feel significant if they are told something in a certain tone of voice or see a certain facial expression. Others feel significant when having their hand held. You can do this indirectly by observing your partner or by directly asking your partner what you can do for them that they would enjoy. It is also a good idea to go over with your partner what you believe are his or her needs. Your partner may feel his/her needs are different from what you believe them to be. Discuss ways for each of you to have your needs met. Remember that a thriving, passionate relationship is rarely based on obedience and conformity to the other's wishes. Romance requires initiative—relationships that are fully alive will usually have the partners looking deeply into each other's needs, finding surprising and passionate ways to serve and even challenge each other. Rank your partner's needs. The 6 Needs are: certainty, uncertainty/variety, significance, love/connection, growth, and contribution.

1.

2.

3.

4.

What are some rules your partner has about having his or her needs met?

Which of these rules make sense? Which of them do not make sense? Do you see any internal contradiction?

Name three ways that you can meet your partner's top needs, even when they are conflicted. How can you use humor and affection to reach your partner?

What kind of feedback from your partner do you need to watch for to let you know you are meeting his or her needs? (Remember you don't necessarily have to require a "thank you."). Get in tune with your partner's needs!

One of life's most gratifying experiences comes from having a passionate and loving relationship with your partner. You can only have this type of relationship if each partner has the honesty, passion, and sufficient independence to create the excitement of diversity and interaction. By keeping an eye open for double-binds, and by holding to a standard of loving honesty, you can experience that pleasure as well.

1. Start with yourself: Find where you're giving double-binds. · What is it that you've been communicating? Explicitly or Implicitly...

2. Where do you feel you are getting double-binds? · Where are you getting the double-binds?

· Without asking your partner, what are they really needing? What's the need underlying the double-bind?

Ask yourself: What's my real message? What do I really need here? Am I looking for love, certainty, significance?

Without asking your partner, what are they really needing? What's the need underlying the double-bind?

Go to your partner and tell them what you really need.

Karen needed both significance/variety (of having a strong, intense man) as well as certainty (of being protected and safe). Doublebinds are a natural result of people trying to reconcile opposite needs and not communicating it well. 3. If you cannot figure out which need is primary, try one of the two injunctions. Do one or the other—to the hilt! Do it fully until you figure out what your partner really wants most.

"Love never dies a natural death. It dies because we don't know how to replenish its source. It dies of blindness, and errors and betrayals. It dies of illness and wounds; it dies of weariness, of witherings, of tarnishings."
—Anais Nin

10

DAY 10: YOU COME FIRST, MY LOVE: THE POWER OF ALIGNMENT

When you are not aligned with your partner, it can seem that all your effort in relationship comes to nothing. When you are aligned, everything you do is reinforced with a greater sense of purpose and fulfillment. In today's session we will explore the Relationship Skill of Uncovering and Creating Alignment. Here we will also learn about the Discipline of Utilization and the Discipline of Gratitude and Giving—these are essential practices for taking the path of growth.

SCORE NEIL ON THE 7 MASTER RELATIONSHIP SKILLS We did not meet Neil's wife until the follow up. But let's challenge ourselves and try to understand how Neil would have scored in the 7 Master Relationship Skills. SKILL 1: HEARTFELT UNDERSTANDING Neil's Score:_____ What understanding did Neil show of his wife's needs? Where did his understanding fall short?

What did he learn?

"Gratitude is not only the greatest of all virtues, but the parent of all the others." —Cicero

SKILL 2: GIVE YOUR PARTNER WHAT THEY REALLY NEED Neil's Score:_____ What were Neil's rules for giving? Which needs did he meet for his wife?

What did she learn? How did he grow?

SKILL 3: CREATE AND BUILD TRUST AND RESPECT Neil's Score:_____ How much trust did Neil create with his wife? What kinds of challenges would you expect to see in a relationship that had that level of trust?

How did Neil change the level of trust in his relationship?

SKILL 4: RECLAIM PLAYFULNESS, PRESENCE, AND PASSION Neil's Score:_____ How did Neil bring playfulness, presence, and passion to the relationship? How did he fail to do that?

What did he learn?

SKILL 5: HARNESS COURAGE AND EMBRACE HONESTY Neil's Score:_____ Was Neil being honest about what his challenge was?

How did Neil show courage? When?

SKILL 6: UNCOVER AND CREATE ALIGNMENT Neil's Score:_____ Why was Neil concerned about his compatibility with his wife?

What did he do about their similarities and their differences?

SKILL 7: LIVE CONSCIOUSLY: BE AN EXAMPLE Neil's Score:_____ Imagine: what preconceptions did Neil have about how to meet his and his wife's needs?

What kind of example was he before? How did that change?

WHAT DID YOU LEARN? POINTS TO REMEMBER ARE YOU COMPATIBLE WITH YOUR PARTNER? When we run into conflicts or misunderstandings with our partner, it is easy to imagine that you are simply not compatible. However, that is usually a fear reaction. Partner compatibility and selection indeed is an important part of relationship success. Once you understand your similarities and your differences from your partner, it is equally important as the skill of uncovering and creating alignment with your partner. This is the bottom-line about compatibility: if you and your partner have one need in common in your top two needs, then an extraordinary relationship is possible. You will still have differences in values, beliefs and rules, but these can be worked with. To begin with, what are your two most valued needs of the 6 Human Needs?

1.

2.

How do you typically meet those needs?

What are your partner's top two needs?

What kind of example was he before? How did that change?

WHAT DID YOU LEARN? POINTS TO REMEMBER ARE YOU COMPATIBLE WITH YOUR PARTNER? When we run into conflicts or misunderstandings with our partner, it is easy to imagine that you are simply not compatible. However, that is usually a fear reaction. Partner compatibility and selection indeed is an important part of relationship success. Once you understand your similarities and your differences from your partner, it is equally important as the skill of uncovering and creating alignment with your partner. This is the bottom-line about compatibility: if you and your partner have one need in common in your top two needs, then an extraordinary relationship is possible. You will still have differences in values, beliefs and rules, but these can be worked with. To begin with, what are your two most valued needs of the 6 Human Needs?

1.

2.

How do you typically meet those needs?

What are your partner's top two needs?

How does he or she typically meet those needs?

What does your partner value in life?

When your partner is happy and productive, describe his or her nature? I s he or she creative, analytical, social, athletic, etc.?

How do you feel about your partner's nature? What do you have in common?

What was your relationship like 6 months in, a year in, two years in?

THE OBJECT OF CONTENTION Do you ever feel that whenever you and your partner disagree, the disagreement always comes back to an old topic you've discussed again and again? Most relationships have one of those—an object of contention. This can get so irritating that you may begin to wonder whether you and your partner are compatible at all! Here you will learn a step-by-step procedure for handling those issues by creating alignment in your relationship. In many relationships, there is an outside interest, a hobby, a friendship, a career, or a habit that is very important to one of the partners. In some cases it can become so important that the other partner begins to feel jealous, to compete with it or try to control it. Take a moment to ask yourself: if there was an outside interest that led to discomfort in your relationship, what would it be? Is it your partner's outside interest, or is it yours? Which of the 6 Human Needs are met by this special interest?

Is there another point of contention in your relationship? A disagreement from long ago that hasn't been resolved? For instance: in how to handle money, how to raise the children, how to spend free time, or what plans are most important for the future?

What do you value most in your relationship? Are you manifesting your values in your relationship?

What do you value most in your special interest or in your point of contention? What does your partner values in his or her special interests or in his or her disagreement with you?

ALIGNMENT STARTS WITH HEARTFELT UNDERSTANDING An object of contention is a long-standing disagreement that has become contentious or even aggressive. In order to avoid senseless conflict, begin resolving the object of contention by putting yourself in your partner's place and gaining heartfelt understanding for his or her experience. Putting yourself in your partner's place can be difficult because if you do it right you may encounter thoughts, feelings or possibilities that you do not want to acknowledge. Now take your spouse's side. FOR SINGLES: Use this exercise to understand a former relationship, or you can use it to understand the issues in another relationship or friendship in your life. Pick a disagreement that has been lingering in the relationship. What is it?

Now score yourself from your partner's perspective. How much certainty is your partner feeling? How much uncertainty, significance, connection, love and contribution? Score these on a scale of 0 to 10. Certainty _____________ Uncertainty/Variety _____________ Significance _____________ Love/Connection _____________ Growth _____________ Contribution _____________ Now what would you do in your partner's position? What are your partner's options in trying to get you to meet his or her needs?

Remember the three levels of relationship? The level of operation in your relationship is the leading indicator of the types of problems, challenges, or benefits you will experience with your partner. 1. Level One: Both partners are looking to get their own needs met without regard for the other's needs. 2. Level Two: The partners focus on fair exchange, you let me pursue mine and I'll let you pursue yours. 3. Level Three: The partners focus on giving to each other unconditionally before any thought of receiving. Think of a point of contention in your relationship and the needs that your partner is trying to meet. What would you do to resolve the point of contention if you were a level one player that is focused on your own needs?

How would you resolve the point of contention if you were a level two player, focused on your needs being "separate but equal?"

How would you resolve the point of contention as a level three player, where you take on your partner's needs as your own?

Do you misinterpret your partner's situation or communications in any way?

How would you score your presence and performance in your relationship?

Do you truly commit and give every ounce of your soul to your partner?

Do you misinterpret your partner's situation or communications in any way?

Out of the Mouths of Babes What would you do on a first date that was turning sour? "I'd run home and play dead. The next day I would call all the newspapers and make sure they wrote about me in all the dead columns." —Craig, age 9

DO IT NOW: DAY 10 ASSIGNMENT YOUR 90-DAY CHALLENGE If you can think of a point of contention in your relationship, or an outside interest that is creating tension, here are some steps that will help resolve the problem and strengthen your relationship. 1. Start by rating how your needs have been met by your partner. On a scale of 1 to 10, rate the levels of certainty, uncertainty/variety, significance, connection/love, growth and contribution. Next, pretend that you are your partner. Rate the levels at which you have been meeting your partner's needs. Now rate how your needs are met by other important parts of your life, in your relationship with a friend, your children, or an outside interest such as a hobby or another activity.

2. Assess your top two needs. What are your top two needs in the relationship? Certainty, uncertainty/variety, significance, connection/love, growth or contribution. What do you value in your relationship? Stability? Love? Excitement? What are your words for it? Now ask yourself, have you been successful at manifesting your values in the relationship? For example, if you value contribution, are you making your partner feel contributed to in the relationship?

3. What comes first? Ask yourself: What comes first for you? Your partner or your other interests? Which have you been putting first in your day-to-day practice? It is easy to take one's partner for granted as one pursues one's interests. How can you change things so that your partner will meet more of your needs at higher levels? What rituals could you put into place together?

Commit and give. If you have chosen to put your partner first, commit to the 90-day challenge, give unconditionally to your partner in every way and in new ways. Watch and learn your partner's needs and what has to happen for him or her to feel their needs are being met. Light up your partner at a level 10 in each of their 6 Needs. Make the next 90 days the greatest 90 days of your partner's life, where no one has given her or him more attention, focus, caring, and love. At the end of the 90 days either you will have lit up your partner and your life will be different or you will know that you truly have different goals, values and direction.

YOUR PARTNER'S 6 NEEDS 1. CERTAINTY a. For Men: make sure that you show up for her emotionally when she is upset. Give her your love and understanding, even if it may not seem welcome in the moment. If she tests you by provoking or criticizing you—take pride and joy in being able to pass that test. Call her on the phone just to tell her that you love her. b. For Women: show him that your love is unconditional. Don't withhold or withdraw from him. Tell him that you will love him forever. Love him as you would love your child, even when he is in a bad mood, even when you're angry and even when he has done something wrong. 2. UNCERTAINTY/ VARIETY a. For Men: take the initiative to surprise her with a special date, flowers or something else that she would especially enjoy. b. For Women: plan a new exciting sexual scenario. Be unpredictable in how and where you show him your love. Tease and provoke him 3. SIGNIFICANCE For both men and women, ask yourself: What could you do on a weekly basis to make her or him feel special? What can you say that will make your partner feel that he or she is the most important person in the world for you? Find three different ways to let her or him know how much they mean to you. 4. LOVE/CONNECTION For both men and women: everybody has different preferred ways for receiving love. Some people respond to touch, others to words. Visual people will respond to a certain look. Others will respond best to gifts and gestures. Discover your partner's preferences and you will be able to give to him or her more effectively with more satisfaction for both of you.

5. GROWTH The way to experience growth in relationship is: a. Commit to each other. Put energy into figuring each other out—learn your partner's needs and learn to cherish his or her individuality, and b. Propose ways that you can grow together toward your goals. 6. CONTRIBUTION First, contribute to each other. When you both feel more fulfilled, you can begin to direct your contribution together in other directions.

Problems are not just problems. They are signs that this is a time for you to grow and contribute. The best way to solve a problem is to strengthen your commitment, to grow and to contribute to the person who matters most to you. Give to your partner like this for 90 days before trying to resolve any points of contention or asking for anything in return. At that point, you will have not only a much greater level of fulfillment, but also much greater clarity about what both of you really need. If you can meet your partner's needs at level nines or tens, and your partner can meet yours, we guarantee that your relationship will be enjoyable and fulfilling!

"Keep love in your heart. A life without it is like a sunless garden when the flowers are dead. The consciousness of loving and being loved brings a warmth and richness to life that nothing else can bring." —Oscar Wild

BONUS DAY: RECLAIMING YOUR TRUE IDENTITY: THE POWER OF VULNERABILITY Whenever we make progress in any area of our life, there's a tendency to backslide. This is because we fail to reward and re-enforce ourselves for making the change, and there are always forces in your environment that will encourage you to play small. As we explore the final Master Relationship Skill, "Live Consciously: Be An Example", we will discover that the skill of being an example requires the awareness of the positive consequences of having high standards and the strength to uphold your new high standards. It is crucial to remember that any change you make, especially in relationships, does not end with you—it creates a chain of positive consequences and examples that will affect thousands or millions of people. If you have children, remember that your example will affect them more than almost any other influence in their lives! And that example in turn will affect their children and so on... forever! Take the responsibility and strength for being fully conscious of the example you set in your life and community!

SCORE LISE ON THE 7 MASTER RELATIONSHIP SKILLS SKILL 1: HEARTFELT UNDERSTANDING Lise's Score:_____ In what areas of life did Lise have heartfelt understanding? Where did she not have it?

What did she learn?

SKILL 2: GIVE YOUR PARTNER WHAT THEY REALLY NEED Lise's Score:_____ What were Lise's rules for giving? What was her style of giving? Did she give strength, or did she take it from people? How?

What did she learn about giving—especially in relation to her son?

What did Lise trust and not trust in herself? What did she learn to trust in herself and in her sister?

SKILL 4: RECLAIM PLAYFULNESS, PRESENCE, AND PASSION Lise's Score:_____ Describe Lise's relationship to playfulness? How did Tony invite her to be playful? What did that do to her femininity?

How would it have affected her relationship with her sister if Lise had let herself be more playful with her? How would playfulness influence her relationships with her sister, husband, and children?

SKILL 5: HARNESS COURAGE AND EMBRACE HONESTY Lise's Score:_____ Describe Lise's capacity for being honest and courageous. For Lise, what other emotions came along with courage? Which emotions did she have to avoid in order to feel courageous?

Did Lise learn any other ways of being courageous? Describe.

SKILL 6: UNCOVER AND CREATE ALIGNMENT Lise's Score:_____ How did Lise find new alignment with her sister?

How did Lise learn to help her son create more alignment with his partner?

SKILL 7: LIVE CONSCIOUSLY: BE AN EXAMPLE Lise's Score:_____ Was Lise consciously creating a new example for those around her, or was she living in reaction to the examples of others?

When she made life changes after the conversation, how did Lise's example change her family? What did Lise have to do to change her family?

Do you ever find yourself wanting to try or do things that just wouldn't be "you?" Have you ever longed to improve relationships with siblings, children or friends but you come up against a barrier whenever you try to stretch for it? If so, it is likely that there was a time in your life when you made a key decision that has shaped how you experience and look at life, and that decision could be affecting not only yourself but also those around you. However, you can make a new decision and open new doors, expanding your ability, your choices and your freedom. What we call our "identity" comes directly from decisions we have made: what we chose to focus on, what skills we developed, how we related to others, and how we want others to see us. Because of influences, conditions, and pressures you experienced you made key decisions that have led you to who you are today. And who you are today influences everyone you love. Yet it is possible to change a key decision that has shaped us even if it's been a part of us for 30 or 40 years. Key decisions direct and command other decisions that you made in your life. There are four qualities that make a decision powerful: 1. The earlier in life the decision is made, the more powerful it will be. 2. The more urgent the circumstances, the more influential the decision. 3. Key decisions set a precedent. 4. A decision gains strength when it is reinforced, leading you to make it again and again. One way to create something new is to go back in time to a past key decision and choose the path you didn't choose before. What you need to do in order to raise the quality of your relationships is to focus attention on the aspects of your life that you have neglected. In this way you will bring balance to your life and to those around you. Key decisions are usually made during moments of crisis. Everybody has had difficult moments in their past and they can often be recalled at a moment's notice. If you reflect on a specific difficult moment in your life, especially in your childhood, you will discover that you made key decisions that perhaps you didn't recognize at the time. While going through difficult circumstances we decide to act, or react in a certain way. These are the decisions that have the most powerful influence over our lives and perhaps it is because they are so powerful that we rarely recognize them as decisions.

Reflect now on a difficult moment in your life. How did you react? Who else was there and how did they react? What kind of decision did you make? Did you decide to be strong and face the challenge, or did you take a position of vulnerability? What were you feeling? Did you decide to trust others, or did you decide to rely on yourself? Or did you put your faith in a set of beliefs or values? Did you focus on your feelings or on other people's behavior, on external circumstances, or did you just want to get away? You may not have thought this out loud at the time, but at the moment you responded to that difficulty, a powerful decision was made. What was it, if you were to state it simply? What did you decide?

That's your key decision. It's not the only one, of course, but you should use that one throughout the rest of this process. When you made your decision, what response did you receive? How did your decision meet your needs at the time? Rate the extent that your needs were met (1-10) and write how your decision met your needs. Certainty ____________ Uncertainty/ Variety ____________ Significance ____________ Love/Connection ____________ Growth ____________ Contribution ____________ Who else was there? How did they react? What were the consequences for them?

Looking back, what other options did you have? What do you think making a different decision would have meant for you? What needs would have been met or not met?

Every key decision affects others in your sphere of influence. It controls an area of your life. Did your key decision affect what your work is today, your family life, your romantic inclinations, your financial habits? Who is affected by that decision? Name the five closest people to you and think of ways that they may have been influenced by your key decision

How many other people have been affected by your key decision indirectly? Think about all the people in your sphere of influence. How many relationships do you have? What other relationships do you influence indirectly?

How have these other people reacted? How have their lives been influenced? What decisions have they made? Have they gone along with your decision, or have they chosen differently? Have you rewarded or punished them for their choices?

Where are their decisions leading them? Where would a different decision lead them? How important is their future to you, rated from 1 to 10.

You are now more aware of the scope of your influence on the lives of those around you. You may even have discovered that people you care about have been hurt by a decision you made long ago. You may also have realized that your key decision served you well within a specific context but that your decision no longer serves you today. You may even have made a key decision recently that may work today but will become a problem for your loved ones later on. If you can see ways that your key decision has led or will lead to some negative side effects for you or others you care about, then it is time to make an adjustment. You must commit to making a change now.

Think of your key decision. Why will you absolutely commit to making a change now?

Consider that at the time your key decision was a "gift." Take a moment to recognize and appreciate the way that your key decision has served you. It probably has led you to develop a set of skills and talents that are yours to keep. What are some of the positive results of your key decision?

Every decision involves excluding possibilities. However, these exclusions are not always accurate. When you made your key decision, what other alternatives did you give up? Was it necessary to give this up? Can you think of anyone else who has made a similar decision without giving up the things that you gave up?

When one person makes a powerful key decision, the people close to them are pushed to grow. How have people around you have been stimulated by your key decision? If you are planning to adjust your key decision, how can you also express your appreciation to those people and for how they have responded to you so far? What would you tell them?

What adjustments could you make to your key decision that would allow you to maintain the benefits of the life you have developed, but also allow you to experience the things that you have sacrificed to this point? Who could benefit if you made this adjustment and reclaimed some of those resources?

How has your key decision affected other people's lives in a negative way? Did it affect your parents, your children, your siblings, or your spouse? What difficulties did they have in relating to you because of your key decision? How may your key decision have affected the way they themselves relate to others? If your key decision has harmed others, it is time to explain to them how this was so and to apologize for any harm you might have caused.

Now it's time for you to strategize specific ways of bringing new experiences to your life and relationships. What could you do now, or soon, to surprise yourself and others? How would that affect your relationships? Make an absolute commitment to action. You have options now. Give them to yourself and decide to enrich your life with them. How are you going to appreciate these new options? How will you communicate them to the people you love?

Imagine now the people in your life that depend on you. Over time, they have developed certain expectations about you. Odds are, however, that they have not seen everything that you are capable of. How can you surprise them? How are you going to reward others in their reactions to your new decision?

Imagine the people who are directly influenced by you and then think of the people who are directly influenced by those individuals. By acting on your full capacity for making decisions, you will be helping others to experience this ability as well. What are the ramifications, even through future generations, of making this change—or yourself and for the others you influence?

The next time you start feeling overwhelmed, ask yourself: · What decision am I dealing with here? · When did I make it? · Why did I make it? · What does it accomplish? · What are its side effects? · What decision could I make now?

DO IT NOW: BONUS DAY ASSIGNMENT 1. How would you have been in relationships before starting this program? How much of each 7 skills? Where were you? How were you showing up? What were you believing was the secret?

Who are you today? What new choices have you made? How are you going to show up from now on? How would you describe what you're going to give in all of your relationships?

Who are you today? What new choices have you made? How are you going to show up from now on? How would you describe what you're going to give in all of your relationships?

How much presence or playfulness or both are you going to bring to the table? How much more fun are you going to have, and why?

Why has relationship transformed for you now, and how have you transformed?

Who are you today? Who were you yesterday? The gap between the two should be something that you're proud of, something you're excited about, and it doesn't have to be perfect. Every move forward you make in relationship creates the opportunity for every other relationship to be moved forward as well.